Contrails

APRIL 13, 2006

To GARY,

A McHENRY

NEIGHBOR + A FRIEND.

Roger T

Contrails

✦

The Memoirs of a Pilot

Roger Thompson

iUniverse, Inc.
New York Lincoln Shanghai

Contrails
The Memoirs of a Pilot

iUniverse, Inc.

For information address:
iUniverse, Inc.
2021 Pine Lake Road, Suite 100
Lincoln, NE 68512
www.iuniverse.com

Front cover photo by Rex Blake Travelstead

Back cover photo by Roger Thompson

Edited by Mary Lou Powers, Carol Ann Powers and Ida Belle Powers

ISBN: 0-595-33691-4

Printed in the United States of America

For Amy, Lisa and Phil.
For Wesley, Lauren, Gracie, Henry
And grandchildren yet unborn…

Contents

1

The Imposter

It was twenty minutes before departure time. I was sitting in the captain's seat of an American Airlines MD-80 jetliner parked at Gate 8 in Springfield, Missouri. Behind me and to the right, I could hear the routine boarding sounds as the passengers filed into the 131-seat aircraft. Flight attendants greeted each traveler, complimenting colorful ties on the men or attractive sweaters on the ladies. Overhead bins slammed shut as passengers stowed their coats and luggage. Friends and strangers fidgeted in nervous excitement.

Those last few minutes before departure are chaotic: food and beverage servicing is completed; seating arrangements are worked out and missing items like soft drinks and coffee cups are located or replaced. During lulls in the passenger parade, the flight attendants chat about job security, family problems or failed relationships. Unfortunately, unless the cockpit door was closed, I heard it all.

Out of the cacophony, I heard a boarding passenger instruct her husband to step into the cockpit. "Tell the captain that you used to be a pilot," she urged. Instinctively, I turned toward the voice and saw a nice-looking man in his late fifties making his way toward me. I think he and his wife were part of a tour group returning from Branson, the new theme park and live-entertainment center in southwest Missouri.

The man stood for a moment in the space between the first officer's seat and mine. Glancing around the cockpit, he seemed to be studying the layout of the various cockpit gauges and switches.

"I heard your wife say that you were a pilot. What did you fly?" I asked him.

"I was a Navy pilot. A-7's," he answered. There was a hint of arrogance in his tone.

"East Coast or West Coast?" I asked him.

During the Vietnam years, the West Coast Navy was charged with the missions to Southeast Asia. The East Coast Navy usually operated in the sunny Mediterranean, making port calls in Italy or Spain.

"West Coast. I did a couple of tours in Vietnam."

"What ship were you on?"

"The Ranger," he said.

"No kidding! Which cruise did you make on the Ranger?"

"We shipped out in the fall of '69."

"I made that cruise, too."

I was stunned—my visitor was describing my own military experience. I was a Navy A-7 pilot who had served on the USS Ranger during her 1969 cruise to Southeast Asia.

I turned to get a closer look at him but he had stepped back and disappeared into the moving crowd. Strange, I thought. A-7 drivers on the Ranger were a small, tight group of just two squadrons: VA-93 and VA-56. The A-7 Corsair was a new aircraft back then, a single-pilot, single-engine Navy carrier aircraft capable of transporting a hefty load of ordnance a considerable distance. The A-7 would even achieve supersonic speeds if the pilot pointed the nose straight down from about 40,000 feet, a normal flight test procedure.

Each A-7 squadron aboard the USS Ranger had 13 or 14 pilots. I knew every pilot on that ship in 1969. But the A-7 guys were like brothers.

There was no time to puzzle over who my passenger might be. The pre-departure routine was complete, the boarding door secured, and we were ready to begin our short flight to St. Louis, about 35 minutes down the road.

After leveling the aircraft at cruising altitude, I made the obligatory informational announcement on the PA about arrival times and weather. As an afterthought, I mentioned that I'd like to speak to the retired Navy pilot on board when we touched down in St. Louis, time permitting. Doubts about his story were still nagging at me, and I thought that perhaps, with a little more conversation, we could discover some shared memories.

After parking the aircraft at Gate D-14 at St. Louis' Lambert International Airport, I popped out of my seat, slipped on my coat and hat and stepped onto the jet bridge to wait for my "Navy buddy." He approached me without hesitation, his wife nowhere in sight.

"Look, that was all a lie," he blurted out. "I flew Navy prop planes for awhile, but I washed out of jet transition. I had trouble keeping up with the airplane."

I paused for a long, awkward moment, allowing his words to sink in.

"Your secret is safe with me," I told him.

He skulked into the terminal like a dog with its tail between its legs. I'm sure his wife had no idea what a phony he was. In fact, he had probably told his story so often that he'd come to believe it. This time, he made the mistake of telling it to the only pilot at American Airlines who was really there, day and night, flying the missions off the deck of the Ranger in 1969. What were the chances that this imposter would tell his story to me?

Later, I was angry. Many stories have been told in recent years of distraught "veterans" at the Vietnam Memorial Wall in Washington, D.C., who, as it turned out, were never anywhere near the Vietnam conflict. In 2003, for example, a professor teaching at Luzerne County Community College in Pennsylvania was humiliated when his claims of being an ex-Navy SEAL and a combat veteran were exposed as lies by real SEALs. He had claimed disability status with the Veteran's Administration and was drawing 100% disability pay, $2367 per month, based on exposure to Agent Orange during close combat in Vietnam. When his fraud was discovered, he committed suicide.

I feel sorry for these cowards who feel the need to invent a personal history to validate their lives. I'm proud of my life, but I don't regard it as extraordinary. I've been privileged to have survived some harrowing experiences and to have met some wonderful, genuine people along the way. I write this book in an attempt to recall the blessings, the luck and the joy that I've known. Of course, aviation stories do get more interesting with age and fighter pilots are notorious liars. But in these pages I've tried to hold fast to the truth. Really.

2

Introduction to Aviation

Life teaches many lessons, many of them unpleasant. For those of us who have survived some of the bumps and bruises along the way, some rules of living reoccur far too often to be random or arbitrary. Some axioms, of course, are overused to the point of becoming clichés. For example: "When one door closes, another one opens." Trite, perhaps, and hardly profound, but that little cliché accurately and thoroughly describes the fateful events that introduced me to my life's work and then guided me safely through thirty-seven years of military and airline flying.

During my junior year at the University of Illinois, I decided that I needed some adventure. I had worked throughout my high school and college years in my uncle's clothing store. It wasn't exciting, but it did finance my education and pay for a small, underpowered Bridgestone motorcycle that served as my fair weather transportation. My uncle, Tony, was the second owner of McGee's Men's Store in McHenry, Illinois. A kinder, wiser boss and friend no one ever enjoyed. He specialized in up-scale brands and grew his business by virtue of his personality and integrity. And along the way, he provided college funds for a series of nephews in need.

My roommate at the university was the son of the editor of the Peoria Journal Star, a Midwestern newspaper of some importance. One day Gus mentioned that all of the newsprint for the Star came from a lumber mill in Canada, at a place called Portage du Ford, Quebec. On a whim, I asked him if his father could get me a summer job as a Canadian lumberjack. "Sure," said Gus.

He was true to his word. At the end of the term, I was on a bus bound for Canada and an adventure that, if I survived, would be memorable. I crated my motorcycle and shipped it via Railway Express to a destination in the north woods that I imagined would be pristine, beautiful and isolated. Portage du Ford may have been all of those things, but I never got the chance to find out.

The bus stopped at the Canadian border between Detroit and Windsor. A very perfunctory Canadian customs official slowly worked his way from the front of the bus to the rear, asking each passenger, in turn, the reasons for his trip and his destination. When he came to me, I announced that I was to be a summer lumberjack at a paper mill in Quebec. He was not impressed.

"Where are your migrant worker's forms?" he inquired.

I had correspondence from the Peoria Journal Star to the lumber mill and a letter of introduction to whomever would be my boss for the summer, but no migrant worker's papers. "Off the bus!" he ordered, and at the ripe old age of 19, I found myself deported from Canada.

A day later, after a humiliating bus ride south, I was at home with my parents in Illinois. I found myself with too much time and absolutely no transportation. My motorcycle was somewhere between Illinois and Quebec, and I wasn't terribly confident that I would ever see it again. My parents, while not openly critical of my misadventure, certainly must have thought me less than sensible. I had no summer job, my savings were minimal and there was still one more unfunded year at the university.

The next afternoon, one of life's doors opened before me…

I was scanning a magazine when I noticed an introductory offer to learn to fly an airplane. "Just present this coupon and five dollars and take a ride…" Hey, why not? I certainly had the time. Now I just had to figure out the transportation.

The following morning, coupon tucked safely in my wallet, I hiked to the outskirts of town, stuck out my thumb (it was a safer world back then), and hitchhiked the 20 miles to Campbell Field, a small, private airport with one paved runway and a couple of grass ones. The fixed base operator, the official term for the owner of all the rental aircraft on the airfield, had a small office in a trailer. I approached a group of clean-cut young men milling around in the vicinity of the trailer and inquired about flight lessons. Someone introduced me to Bill Collier, a tall, thin, young man with a blunt manner and a steady gaze. Bill was working as an instructor, acquiring flight experience with an eye toward landing an airline job. I gave him five dollars and my coupon, and the next thing I knew, I was making the acquaintance of a certain blue and white Cessna 150 aircraft that was parked just a short walk from the trailer complex.

Bill began the introductory flight with a tour of the outside of the Cessna and the safety checks necessary for preflight. Then we climbed into the front seats. He started the engine, taxied to the runway, shoved the throttle fully forward and accelerated into the sky. The smile on my face started on the take-off roll and remained stupidly fixed for the next thirty minutes. He demonstrated turns, climbs, stalls, and finally, landings. What a blast! By the time he parked that little Cessna, I was hooked!

"Sign me up," I said. "What do I have to do next?"

Bill explained that there are several categories of Federal Aviation Association licenses and medical certificates. To be certified to carry passengers in flight, one must have a minimum of a private pilot's license and a second class medical certificate. He told me that I would have to see an FAA-approved doctor to get the medical certificate. The private license would take a minimum of forty hours of flight experience, some of which would be with an instructor and some would be solo practice time. The cost was trivial by today's standards, but in 1966, to an unemployed college student with an emaciated savings account, it was considerable: $8/hour to rent the airplane; $4/hour for the instructor.

I managed to find a job working nights at a local factory degreasing radiator parts. During the day, I'd hitchhike to Campbell Field for flight lessons. Somehow, I managed to jump through all of the medical and FAA hoops and by the end of the summer, I had passed the first flight examination of my aviation career. I was the proud owner of a private pilot certificate. And, God, was I proud!

Miraculously, my motorcycle appeared at the end of July and my transportation situation became infinitely less complicated.

Incidentally, an occurrence on my second flight at Campbell Field turned into a personal aviation tradition that was observed throughout my military and airline careers. For some odd reason, every second flight in a new airplane precipitated an unusual and sometimes life-threatening in-flight situation. I've survived fires, smoky cockpits, radio failures, mid-air collisions, loss of pneumatic pressure and landing gear problems, but always on that second flight. As Bill Collier and I were making the final approach and landing of my "first" second flight in the Cessna 150 in 1966, I caught sight of an orange blur coming at us from below. We felt the impact as a radio-controlled model airplane collided with the leading edge of our left wing and then splattered itself on the tail, leaving behind black rubber streaks and orange paint. It was an initiation, of sorts, to what was yet to come.

By the end of the summer, I felt confident enough in my navigation and flying skills to attempt a long, cross-country trip. I threw a sleeping bag and some extra clothes behind the seats of my favorite Cessna, checked the weather, filed a flight plan and took off from Campbell Field. Next stop: Phoenix. Well, not exactly. A little Cessna 150 can't fly very far on a tank of gas, so I hop-scotched across the Midwest from airport to airport, refueling my plane and my stomach, monitoring enroute weather at the local flight service stations. I spent one night curled up under a wing on the tarmac in Dalhart, Texas. One of the locals told me that someone had killed a rattlesnake about fifty feet from where I was sleeping.

About a hundred miles east of Phoenix, looking down from an altitude of 8,000 feet, I saw a silver blur moving at a fantastic speed. I could tell that it was an airplane, obviously a jet, and it was about to impact upon a rocky foothill right below me. I reached for my map, thinking that I needed to determine my exact position so that I could report the site of the crash when it occurred. As I watched, the silver blur raced toward the hill. At the last possible instant, it skimmed the hill, soared straight up in front of my nose and disappeared above me, leaving me feeling that I was suspended in mid-air and stationary. What a kick it must have been to fly something so fast and maneuverable! I think that something was born in me at that moment, something filed away in my subconscious which would one day entice me into the world of speed, aerial freedom and exhilaration.

I spent a few days in Phoenix with my aunt and uncle, giving airplane rides and probably showing off. On a whim, my uncle and I decided to fly to Las Vegas, a 250 mile trip over uninhabited desert. We flew along, chatting amiably, enjoying the scenery and landed without incident at one of the small airports circling Las Vegas. We found something to eat, refueled the trusty Cessna and started back for Phoenix.

By now, the light was failing as the sun settled behind mountain ranges to our west. We were flying southeasterly, between two ridge lines, both of which exceeded the altitude capabilities of a Cessna 150. It had been so easy in the daylight to stay between those ridgelines, but at night, I was rapidly discovering how dark the desert could be. After a very short time, our granite boundaries disappeared into the moonless night and I was forced to navigate using a compass heading and navigational radio beacon broadcasting somewhere ahead of us. What a quiet return trip we had! My uncle knew the mountains were there. He had seen them disappear as I had. We flew along in silence, neither one of us willing to verbally acknowledge the rocky hazards to our left and right.

I was reminded of the favorite saying of one of my first flight instructors: "There are old pilots and there are bold pilots. But there are no old, bold pilots." For a time, over that dark, deserted desert I was convinced that I would never achieve old or bold status as a pilot. Fortunately, the lights of Phoenix came into view and broke the tension in the cockpit. My uncle never told me exactly what he thought of that trip from Las Vegas to Phoenix. And I never asked.

Sometimes I think back to that episode on the bus at the U.S.-Canadian border. What if I had lied to that Canadian customs official and told him that I was on my way to spend the summer with my Aunt Ruth in Toronto? I wonder if I would have survived the chain saws, sawmills and knife fights of the north woods. How different my life would have been had I not been available when the aviation opportunity presented itself. The door that locked me out of the great Canadian wilderness forced me to discover the hidden entrance to civilian and military flying and a series of challenging, entertaining adventures.

Very soon, the local draft board would continue the tradition of opening and closing the doors of my life…

3

The Draft

The military draft of the 1960s was an arbitrary, malevolent, despised black cloud hovering over the nation's college and university students. College students, who were in the prime age group to become cannon fodder for the Vietnam war, fomented vocal anti-war demonstrations, sit-ins, protests and other sometimes bloody confrontations with authorities. Everyone on campus had a student deferment that delayed entry into the military for the four years of undergraduate study. Additional deferments were available in certain circumstances. Graduate school was the first choice of those who could afford it. Former president Bill Clinton, for example, avoided the draft by studying in Oxford, England. Sylvester Stallone, who would earn millions portraying the Vietnam hero, Rambo, successfully avoided military service. Selected industries, arbitrarily classified as critical, petitioned local draft boards to permanently exempt their employees from military duty. Some young men declared themselves conscientious objectors. Still others sought sanctuary in Canada.

The students attending the University of Illinois, where I was an undergraduate, participated in anti-Vietnam war demonstrations, but the protests were much less violent than the ones at Kent State and Berkeley. The draft and the ongoing war in Vietnam were somewhere in the back of my consciousness in the fall of 1966 as I began my senior year at the university, but the government letter that arrived in early October caught me completely by surprise. "Greetings," it began. I had been drafted.

I reported for an Army physical in the Chicago area and was pronounced fit for duty. I contacted the Air Force and Navy recruiters, seeking alternatives to the Army, preferably as a pilot. If I had to go to war, my weapon of choice was an airplane, not a rifle. I successfully passed the Air Force and Navy pilot aptitude tests and scheduled appointments for the respective physical exams.

The Air Force physical was a disaster. The general examination was routine until it came time to give a blood sample. I have always found the sight of my own blood unsettling. The corpsman tasked to draw a vial of blood may have

9

been having a bad day, or he might have been new at his job, or maybe he just didn't like me, but he stabbed my arm five times before the blood began to flow. On that fifth time, the blood burst out of my arm and splattered all over the wall. It had been a long time since I'd eaten lunch and a nasty headache had been incubating for some time. Seeing the blood on the wall—my blood—put me over the edge. By now, my head was pounding and I was slightly woozy.

The next stop on the assembly line physical was the vision test. I stood the required distance from the eye chart, my toes behind the line painted on the floor. I could barely see the wall, however, much less the chart. Needless to say, the Air Force didn't invite me to become one of its premier pilots.

The Navy physical was administered at the Naval Air Station in Glenview, a northern Chicago suburb. I thought that the exam had gone well, but I was notified sometime later that I had failed one of the required vision tests. The Navy offered me a slot as a flight officer—a navigator—not a pilot. I arranged for a retest, and this time I passed. Afterward, I was interviewed by a civilian who was wearing a business suit. We must have talked about many things but the only question I recall, some 35 years later, was how I felt about going to Vietnam as a Navy pilot. I replied that I had no reservations. At the time, I hadn't considered the consequences of fighting as a naval aviator. I was focused solely on avoiding the Army draft. My army experience, limited to time spent in the endless queues of the draft physical and the nightly TV news body count reports of the jungle fighting, motivated me to seek alternatives to army service. It hadn't occurred to me that dying in the skies over Vietnam would be just as permanent as death in its jungles.

Within a week, I received a letter from the Navy ordering me to report for Aviation Officer Candidate School in mid-February, subject to the completion of my degree at the university. I knew that if I missed that class date, the Army would scoop me up before the Navy gave me a second chance. My Army induction date was scheduled for May. It was now late October and I had less than four months until the end of the semester.

Panic is a wonderful motivator. I discovered that if I changed my course of study from a straight physics major to a liberal arts and sciences physics major and added another two-hour course to my work load, I would have just enough credits to graduate at the end of the semester, my seventh semester at the University of Illinois. I begged a friendly professor in the music department to give me private lessons in percussion for that magic two hours. Somehow, the plan came together. Miraculously, my final exam in quantum mechanics was sufficient to transform a failing grade into a "C," and I was on my way to Pensacola. And another door was opening…

4

Pensacola

Naval Air Station Pensacola, Florida, is home to naval aviation. Every naval aviator has spent time in Pensacola and most remember it fondly.

In February of 1967, I reported to Pensacola as a member of Aviation Officer Candidate Class 0767, the seventh class of 1967. For the next four months, life was a *mélange* of screaming Marine drill instructors, swim classes, physical training, classroom instruction, wonderful and abundant food with little time to eat it, running, close-order drill and panic. It was boot camp designed for young college men who were aspiring to be naval aviators and officers.

Fortunately, I was a fair swimmer before Pensacola. The Navy expects its pilots to be comfortable and proficient in any conceivable aquatic situation so we were drilled unmercifully in survival techniques. We were required to jump from a twenty-foot tower and swim underwater for what seemed like miles without breaking the surface. The intention of the exercise was to simulate escape from a burning ship engulfed in flaming liquid. For this purpose, we were dressed in baggy flight suits and tennis shoes. My flight suit was so much larger than I that it trapped a large bubble of air when I jumped feet first into the water. It took so much energy to fight the buoyancy of the inflated flight suit that I had trouble swimming the required distance underwater and my butt would break the surface some distance from the finish line. Every time my butt popped up, the instructors counted it as a failure and back to the tower I would go. Finally, I hyperventilated to a point just shy of unconsciousness, took the leap and swam successfully.

Another water torture was the distance swim. Swimming a mile, under recreational conditions, can be enjoyable. But when you're dressed in that baggy flight suit and tennis shoes and you're swimming laps with fifty of your buddies flailing over and around you, any element of fun is gone.

And then, of course, there is the Dilbert Dunker, a mock-up of a cockpit that slides down rails into the pool, flips upside down and sinks. The purpose of this exercise is to overcome underwater disorientation and panic. Wearing a baggy flight suit, gym shoes and a pilot's helmet, each officer candidate climbs into a "cockpit" that is perched precariously on rails that tilt toward the water at a 45 degree angle. A seat belt and shoulder harness assembly are maliciously tightened on the victim and he is given a few seconds to consider his fate. Then an instructor flips a switch and the cockpit begins its sickening acceleration down the rails and slams into the water. Heart in his throat and panic on his mind, the officer candidate is supposed to let the bubbles dissipate, figure out which direction is up, calmly disconnect his harness apparatus and swim free from the sinking, inverted cockpit. Once you figure out the routine, it becomes a fun ride. But the first time down the rails is sheer panic.

In May of 1967, I was commissioned an ensign in the United States Navy. My parents flew in for the occasion and I went AWOL to pick them up at the airport. Fortunately, nobody noticed that I was gone.

After commissioning, we moved into the Bachelor Officer Quarters for the next phase of training. The buildings, I'm sure, were pre-World War II, but after the barracks life of officer candidate school, it was good to have a private room, however sparse. For entertainment, I could always turn on the overhead light in my BOQ room late at night. For an instant, a squadron of huge cockroaches would freeze in the center of the floor like guilty children caught in the act. Then they would scatter at high speed to their individual hiding places, invisible again, unless something strategic in the room was moved.

Aviation ground school occupied the next couple of weeks. We studied aerodynamics, mathematics, weather and assorted naval topics, subjects that finally hinted that we may soon be flying airplanes. The ground instructors gave us an overview of the flight training syllabus and explained how the selection process worked. Obviously, flight school would not be available if we didn't pass the comprehensive test on the ground school subjects. But, after that, flight grades in primary training were governing. Students would be ranked on the basis of the scores they earned flying the T-34 Mentor and awarded their areas of naval aviation in descending order. Routinely, there were about ten slots available for jet training and the rest of the class of sixty young ensigns would be divided between naval propeller aircraft and helicopters. I wanted to fly jets, as did a good chunk of my classmates. The competition would be tough.

The final ground school test was given on a Friday afternoon. It was straightforward and not terribly difficult. Some time later, the entire class congregated around a newly posted list assigning each student to an individual flight instructor. Scuttlebutt had it that one instructor was to be avoided at all costs: Lieutenant Jim Sanders, who was notorious for a vile temper and low flight grades.

Whoever was unlucky enough to draw Lt. Sanders was doomed to fly helicopters for his Navy career.

When I finally elbowed my way close enough to the list to find my name, my heart fell. Ensign Thompson was assigned to Lt. Sanders. Training started Monday morning. Good-bye jets.

Bright and early Monday morning, dressed in Navy-issue flight suit and boots, I shook Lt. Sanders' hand.

"Have you ever flown an airplane?" he asked me.

"Yes, sir. I have a private pilot's license."

"Good. I picked you," he said. "You had good grades in ground school and you're going to be Student of the Week, the top flight student."

I didn't know what to say. Obviously, he was setting me up for something but I didn't have the first idea where he was going. It didn't really matter, I guess. At this point I had given up all hope and was just along for the ride.

Lt. Sanders and I walked out to our waiting aircraft, a T-34, the military version of the Beech Bonanza, a single engine propeller trainer with fore and aft seating. I climbed into the front seat, he settled in the back, and we began that first flight. Once airborne, he asked me over the intercom if my seatbelt was tight.

"Yes, sir," I told him.

Immediately, he flipped the aircraft inverted. I was left dangling, my hands and feet too distant from the controls to have any input and my head bumping on the canopy. It was a lesson that I never forgot. In the future, if my seatbelt wasn't painfully tight, I didn't feel comfortable in an airplane, whether it was a jet fighter or an airliner.

The rest of the flight was uneventful. We landed, taxied to parking and went inside to one of the briefing rooms. We spent some time talking about what had occurred in flight and how I could improve my performance. At no time did I even catch a glimpse of the temper for which Lt. Sanders was infamous. Finally, he showed me the grades he was going to post for this introductory lesson. They were perfect! Superlatives in every category. I was astounded, but grateful.

And that's how the flight syllabus progressed. Lt. Sanders would instruct in the calmest of demeanors. I would learn and demonstrate my progress. And the grades were always perfect. Only once did I see his temper flare. I don't remember my offense but the voice that erupted from the back seat of that T-34 seared my backside and reddened my ears.

By the way, during my second flight in that T-34, the flap motor underneath my seat caught on fire and the cockpit filled with smoke. The second flight jinx continued.

At the end of primary Navy flight training, I had earned the best grades in the class and was, indeed, chosen Student of the Week. I was awarded one of the coveted jet slots and was told to report for basic jet training at NAS Meridian, Mississippi.

Although I can never be certain, I think I know why Lt. Sanders treated me as he did. I speculate that by virtue of his naked temper, he had established such a negative reputation as an impossible instructor that he needed someone to redeem himself. He needed to be able to point to a success story, a student under his tutelage who had excelled. I was the lucky guy.

5

Mishaps

Naval aviation is, by definition, dangerous. Formation flying, weapons delivery, air combat maneuvering, in-flight refueling, catapulted take-offs and arrested landings are not the stuff of recreational pilots. It is inevitable that casualties of men and machines will occur during the learning process.

The Navy encourages incompetent or unmotivated aviators to quit early in the flight-training program. Dropped on Request (DOR) is the official term used to describe officers who decide they would rather walk than fly.

Frequently, after a fatal training accident, a number of students decide to go DOR. The married flight students are especially vulnerable. After listening to their wives chip away at them about the prospects of widowhood or single motherhood, their self-confidence can be mortally wounded. To keep peace in the family, many of them quit, usually on a Monday morning after a long weekend discussion with their wife and family. Being unmarried during flight training has its advantages.

One friend of mine dropped out of the flight program because he could never quite master instrument flight. Another became airsick every time he flew and ultimately quit. The Navy's message to those unsuited to the challenge was: "Quit, and the sooner the better!"

It was not a malevolent policy. The Navy knew that training demands would become increasingly difficult, culminating with the night landing qualification aboard an aircraft carrier. They reasoned that it was more humane and economical to terminate a sub-par aviator before he killed himself, and others, and to avoid the potential damage to military or civilian property.

The financial cost of training a pilot was another consideration that figured prominently in the Navy's planning. In 1967, the government spent a million dollars to train each jet pilot to proficiency and reminded us of that fact daily.

The aircraft carrier is the heart and soul of naval aviation. With a crew of 5,000, it can project the power and might of the United States on short notice to an area of the world in need of stabilization or punishment. It is an awesome weapon. But the carrier, with its 70,000 tons of bulk steel and four acre flight deck, is totally dependent on the 130 operational pilots who fly its combat aircraft in all types of weather, in daylight and in darkness, operating from a pitching flight deck, carrying the fight to the enemy. To become a Navy carrier pilot, one must master the most challenging, the most difficult and dangerous role in modern aviation. Training for that role is serious business.

I received my Navy wings in July of 1968 after completing advanced jet training in Beeville, Texas. What a place! The water was corrosive enough to eat your car instead of clean it, the summer heat and humidity were routinely in the high 90's and the tarantulas traveled in herds. John Freitag, a future California roommate of mine, discovered a lone tarantula in the parking lot one day. He happened to have his hunting knife with him and decided to impale the large black beast. After it jumped as high as John's head, he decided to leave it alone.

In our graduating class, John ranked number one and I was number two. I think there were more than two pilots in the class, but I can't be sure. We were both assigned to West Coast A-7's, our first choice. Lemoore, California, here we come!

The A-7 Replacement Air Group (RAG) in Lemoore was the last training stop for a pilot before he was assigned to an operational A-7 Corsair squadron. The RAG trained fully qualified naval aviators of diverse backgrounds to become proficient A-7 pilots. The syllabus included ground school, of course, simulator emergency procedures, instrument refresher training, conventional and nuclear weapons training, air combat maneuvering, day and night carrier landing qualification and terrain-following radar navigation. It was an ambitious syllabus, but the A-7 was a wonderful new airplane. I felt honored to be among the first group of Navy pilots trained to fly it.

Since the Corsair is a single-pilot airplane, my first flight in it was solo. But the procedures trainer and the simulator were adequate to help me develop a feel for the way it flew and I knew my first flight would be just dandy. It was the second flight that I was concerned about. On that second flight, my radio failed and the landing gear would not extend. My jinx continued.

On March 18th, 1969, I was scheduled for an air combat maneuvering flight, a lesson in high-speed, air-to-air tactics known affectionately among fighter pilots as "dog-fighting". Flown aggressively by physically fit, competitive pilots, dog-fighting is a three-dimensional, high-speed, heavy g-loading attempt to maneuver your aircraft to the rear of your opponent's plane and keep it there for a missile or gun shot. It was not unusual to pull seven g's during the hard turns as we fought to cut inside an opponent's turning radius. In other words, a 150-pound pilot might weigh seven times that, or 1050 pounds, as he fought the centrifugal force of a high-speed turn.

My opponent would be an instructor pilot flying an A-4 Skyhawk, a small, extremely maneuverable single-engine jet with a delta wing and a mean turning radius. I can't recall the name of that A-4 pilot whom I "fought" that day. I should have remembered him. He saved my life.

The hour before our scheduled flight we spent briefing every aspect of the training mission we were about to fly, with a heavy emphasis on the tactics and maneuvers of high-speed jet combat. At the speeds we would be operating, it was extremely easy to lose sight of your opponent, thereby forfeiting any advantage in the fight.

The practice area we would be using was east of Visalia, California, in the foothills of the Sierras, isolated from general aviation traffic. 20,000 feet was to be our maximum altitude, to keep us below and away from all high-altitude airliners.

After the take-off from Lemoore Naval Air Station, we flew in loose formation to the practice area, the Skyhawk in the lead. When my instructor was satisfied the area around us was clear, he signaled me to climb to a position 2,000 feet above him and 100 yards off his right wing. When I was stabilized in position, he radioed that the fight was on!

I banked 135 degrees to the left, lowered the nose and kicked left rudder, maneuvering toward his tail. He turned into me and I reversed the bank, pulling hard as I passed behind his tail and through his jet wash.

Most airline passengers have experienced jet wash, but at a substantial distance from the source. The sudden, heart-dropping jolt as one airliner passes through the wake of another, miles away, can be disconcerting, but hardly dangerous. The turbulent air exiting the tail cone of a jet engine could be compared to the wake of a speedboat. Water vapor, one of the by-products of combustion, exits the jet engine at a high velocity and temperature. At high altitudes, where the outside air temperature routinely approaches -40 degrees Fahrenheit, the condensation trails (contrails) freeze very quickly into ice clouds to form those distinctive lines across the sky.

In addition to the turbulence produced by the engine, each wing tip of an aircraft produces vortices, tornado-like violent disruptions of the airflow. The vortex from the left wing rotates clockwise as it leaves the wing tip and the vortex from the right wing rotates counterclockwise. The combination of wing tip vortices and engine wake produce the phenomenon known as jet wash.

The interaction of jet wash and the high elevator load on my aircraft (I was pulling hard on the controlstick, trying to minimize my turn radius) produced a violent nose-down reaction that pitched me forward in my shoulder straps. I realized that the aircraft had experienced an accelerated stall even though my airspeed was around 390 miles per hour. My Corsair assumed a 35 degree nose-down attitude and began rolling over and over to the left, losing altitude rapidly.

There is a procedure for recovery from a full stall condition in the A-7. I disconnected the control-stick steering input from the autopilot, released the controls, and retarded the throttle to idle. The A-7 has a mechanism whereby the autopilot "remembers" the inputs of the pilot and augments the controls as he manually flies the airplane. Once that control-stick steering is disconnected and any pro-spin-control inputs by the pilot are released, the airplane is supposed to fly itself out of the stall. No dice.

I grabbed the controlstick in an attempt to manually right the aircraft, which was spinning even more violently than before. It was difficult to read any of the instruments because the aircraft was rotating so rapidly, but I knew that my altitude was dangerously low. My mind was racing...there was no time for fear. I was consumed with the task of righting my aircraft and returning it to normal flight.

Fortunately, the A-4 pilot had kept my gyrating airplane in sight. As he watched me drop lower and lower toward the mountains, he made up his mind.

"Get out of it!" he radioed.

I reached behind my head for the face-curtain handle of the ejection seat and pulled it with both hands. The seat fired with about a 1-second delay and I found myself tumbling in free space, my aircraft somewhere below me and my left arm blown backwards. I brought my arm forward and reached for the "D" ring of my parachute. At that instant, the chute deployed automatically with a violent jerk. I looked up and saw a perfect parachute canopy above me. I released one corner of my oxygen mask, deployed the survival kit and raft from my seat pack and lifted my visor. I could see the fireball where the aircraft had crashed.

As I slowly descended, drifting east with the wind, I could see the rolling hills and scattered pine trees of the Sierra foothills. There was a deserted building situated next to a pond to the southwest of me and a high, snow-covered ridge to the east. I forced myself to think of the challenges yet to come and ignored the violence of the past few seconds.

I mentally reviewed the procedures for a parachute landing. Ages ago, I had joined parachute clubs in Illinois and Mississippi and learned proper landing techniques. I never made a jump with those clubs, however, because the winds were always too strong for a novice. I guess I was finally getting my chance.

Oxygen was still flowing through my face-mask from the emergency bottle in the pan of the ejection seat still attached to my harness. I was concerned that if I reattached the mask to my helmet and was knocked unconscious on landing, I would suffocate when the emergency supply ran out. I detached the mask from the seat pan, removed the clip from the other side of my helmet, and let it fall.

About a hundred feet above the ground, I brought my feet together and placed my hands on the parachute risers. I landed on the bank of a stream on wet, packed sand next to a tree and a brush pile. The chute came down and deflated in the tree. I released the coke fittings that fastened the parachute to my torso harness, climbed out of my gear and piled all unnecessary equipment into the inflated raft that had been dangling below me during my descent.

Feeling very much alive and invigorated, I walked over to a clearing and flashed the Skyhawk with my signal mirror to let him know that I was OK. He appeared to have seen me so I went back to the parachute and pulled it out of the tree. I placed it in the clearing so that its orange panels would be highly visible.

After about fifteen minutes, the A-4 disappeared. I figured that he must have returned to the base. I could hear other jets circling but they were above the overcast that had moved in and I couldn't get a look at them.

A farmer came over one of the hills and asked if I was all right. He offered to give me a ride somewhere, but I figured that a helicopter was probably on the way. I asked him to call the Lemoore Naval Air Station, tell them my position and let them know that I was fine.

Soon after the farmer left, the A-4 showed up again, flying below the overcast. I signaled to him with a smoke flare. He circled my position, staying close, like a noisy guardian angel. About an hour after the ejection, a Navy search and rescue helicopter lumbered in and landed across the hill from me. I left all of my discarded gear in the raft, climbed aboard the helo and flew back to Lemoore.

I spent a couple of hours at the Navy hospital where the good doctors pronounced me none the worse for the wear. I was probably a couple of inches shorter than I had been after riding the two-stage rocket of that ejection seat. Somebody in authority suggested that I call home to tell my folks that I wasn't dead, since the national news had been running the story of my ejection—it must have been a slow news day.

Initially, the investigation into the cause of the accident leaned heavily toward pilot error. But then, in combing through the maintenance records of the ruined aircraft, it was discovered that a flight control modification should have been performed on all the early A-7s to prevent the control-stick steering mechanism from adding pro-stall inputs during a full stall condition. Guess which airplane never received the modification? This neglected maintenance procedure also explains why the stall recovery procedure didn't work—-the airplane was working against itself.

The Navy wanted me back in the cockpit as soon as possible. My log book indicates that six days after the crash I flew another A-7 for almost two and a half hours. It felt great.

My use of the ejection seat was the textbook way to escape from a doomed aircraft in flight. What my fellow trainee, Ron Yenzer, did a couple of months later was not only unique; it was terrifying.

On May 6th, 1969, I was a member of a group of naval aviators aboard the USS Lexington, off the coast of San Diego. We were scheduled for the final phase of RAG training: day and night A-7 carrier qualification. This would be my first exposure to night carrier operations, the most difficult and frightening aspect of naval aviation.

May 6th had been a busy day. I had completed seven catapulted take-offs and seven arrested landings, all during daylight hours. The A-7 was an honest, stable aircraft around the ship, responding well to changes in power, attitude or line-up. But that was in daylight. At night, scary things happen.

Later, on the first instrument approach of the evening, I talked to myself as I flew toward the ship and my first night landing, or trap. What an exercise in panic-control! By the time the evening was over, however, I had three night carrier landings and three night cat shots to my credit. Three more night traps and my RAG syllabus would be complete.

The next day I logged three more day landings and cat shots. Landing aboard the ship during the daytime was great fun! My confidence was at an all-time high. Just those last three night traps to go.

As the pinkish-orange sunset of the eastern Pacific was fading into night, the Lexington turned into the wind, the catapult fired and I was airborne for the first of my three night approaches. I noticed that fog was slowly decreasing visibility around the ship and the cloud ceiling was moving lower. With each subsequent approach and landing, the weather deteriorated. By the time I made my final approach, I could barely see the flight deck from three-quarters of a mile away. Fortunately, my tail hook caught an arresting cable and my night was complete!

I taxied forward on the bow, parked the aircraft, and held the brakes until the deck crew installed the tie-down chains. Then I shut down the engine. Exhausted, I dragged myself out of the cockpit and staggered to the ready room, the combination pilot lounge and squadron headquarters several levels below the flight deck. By now, there was only one airplane still airborne: Ron Yenzer on his final approach of the evening.

Ron Yenzer was a slightly built young man. Quiet and unassuming, he was the antithesis of the stereotypical fighter-pilot personality. But Ron was about to be tested.

When I walked into the ready room, I found that all of my hot and sweaty buddies had congregated around the PLAT TV in one corner of the room. The PLAT is a closed-circuit camera mounted in the flight deck, in the vicinity of the arresting cables. It looks up the glide slope at the descending, landing aircraft. From the audio, we could tell that Ron was very close to the ship, but because of the poor visibility, we couldn't see him. Then, suddenly, there he was. Just a few feet above touchdown, he had broken out of the fog and looked to be in a good position to land. But as we watched, now from the camera that overlooks the flight deck, we could see that Ron was in trouble.

He touched down in the landing area, and his hook caught a wire. But instead of decelerating straight down the angled deck, his aircraft rapidly drifted left and pitched over the side of the ship. The aircraft came to rest with its nose pointing straight down at the water, still dangling from the hook that was tenuously attached to the ship's arresting cable. The engine roared at full power. The stubby A-7 hook held for a brief moment before it released the cable, sending Ron and his machine into the depths, like a jet-propelled submarine.

The Pacific Ocean at night, in the fog, is a dark and frightening place. When Ron Yenzer's Corsair entered the water, his engine immediately died and his cockpit lights were extinguished. He knew he was sinking, and in his quiet, cool way, he reviewed his options. He decided to take the quickest way out. He pulled the handle that set the ejection process into motion.

Never designed as an underwater escape mechanism, the McDonnell Douglas ejection seat, in a finely timed sequence of events, jettisons the Plexiglas cockpit canopy, blasts the seat assembly out of the cockpit, separates the pilot from that seat and deploys the parachute. What actually happened when Ron pulled the handle underwater, no one will ever know for sure. He remembers being hopelessly tangled in parachute cord, struggling to extricate himself in the cold, inky water. The oxygen bottle, still attached to his seat pan, allowed Ron to breathe for a time, but his exertions quickly used it up and he began to drown.

Just before he lost consciousness, he became aware that something had buoyed him out of the water. Perhaps he had flailed his way back to the tail while the airplane rolled and twisted underwater, belching up the air that was trapped within it. Maybe when the nose pitched down, the tail briefly sprang up, carrying Ron with it. All he knew at the time was that he had a second chance to live.

He grabbed his knife and cut away the cords that were binding him to the airplane just as it receded into the depths. He inflated his Mae West life preserver, found his flashlight and signaled to the search and rescue helicopter hovering nearby. And then, with a little help from the crew of the SAR helo, he was hoisted aboard and flown back to the Lexington, shivering and wet, but alive.

Two nights later, Ron Yenzer completed his final night-qualification. He was soon assigned to an operational squadron and went on to serve two tours of duty in Vietnam, just as I did.

The mishaps Ron and I experienced were certainly not unique. Unusual, perhaps, but a fairly typical representation of some of the hazards faced by naval aviators as they train to proficiency in a very dangerous, but exciting, profession.

6

Survival Schools

The Navy flight program emphasized survival on both land and sea. The United States Government was spending a tremendous number of taxpayer-dollars teaching us to fly expensive airplanes that we would employ in dangerous situations. Survival training was an insurance policy on their investment. Water survival training, begun when we were officer candidates, continued throughout active duty. Land survival schools were thrown into the syllabus at odd intervals, depending upon deployment schedules and the needs of the service.

Water to the Navy pilot is sanctuary. Given a choice, a naval aviator would prefer to nurse a mortally wounded airplane out to sea where he could be rescued by his comrades rather than eject over enemy territory. Running around in the jungle, hoping to be rescued by friendly commandos, was never something to which I aspired.

The most comprehensive water survival school that I attended was located at San Diego, California. Outfitted in flight suits, tennis shoes and cast off helmets, we were ferried in groups of fifteen out to sea. Our vessel was a flat top boat modified for the purpose: at the aft end, scaffolding supported a wooden platform, roughly fifteen feet above the deck and perhaps twenty feet above the water. Above the platform was a set of metal guides over which parachute shroud lines were run. The craft cruised at a steady six knots, riding the swells of the Pacific Ocean.

We were issued torso harnesses similar to the ones we used to strap ourselves into our A-7 cockpits. The harnesses were equipped with the survival gear normally contained in the seat pan of the ejection seat.

When it was my turn, I climbed the scaffolding to the platform where an efficient but sadistic chief petty officer waited. He connected the overhead shroud lines from the boat to my harness and instructed me to stand facing him on the aft edge of the platform. When he felt the urge, he gave me a mighty shove and I fell backwards, dropping the twenty feet to the water, simulating a parachute water entry. The boat continued forward, pulling me by the shroud lines that were attached to my torso harness. The procedure simulated being dragged at sea by a wind-driven parachute, but I felt more like baitfish on a line.

I crossed my legs and moved my hands up on the risers, as I had been taught in the water survival ground school. Immediately, the forward motion flipped me over on my back and I was able to get my head up and out of the water. I spat out the salt water that had been forced into my nose and mouth while being dragged face down through the waves. I ran my hands up the risers, searching for the quick-disconnect fittings. When I found them, I simultaneously squeezed both release buttons and freed myself from the boat that was intent on dragging me to Hawaii. I settled into the water and relaxed as it motored over the horizon, leaving me in solitude, riding the undulating swells of the Pacific Ocean.

The first order of business was to improve my buoyancy. I inflated my Mae West and instantly bobbed higher in the water. Relieved of the requirement to keep my head above the waves, I retrieved the lanyard attached to my torso harness that led to the water survival package. With some difficulty, I pulled the red handle that inflated my one-man raft and clambered aboard. I felt like I was finally getting control of the situation.

By the time I had inventoried the other toys in the survival kit (signal flares, sea dye marker, desalination kit for drinking water, condoms for water storage and shark repellant, affectionately known as hamburger helper), I was joined by another pilot who had been jettisoned from the SS Sadistic. By early afternoon a dozen abandoned Navy pilots floated together in a loose circle on their private rafts, telling jokes and trying to get the desalination kits to produce some drinkable water.

Just before sundown, we heard the helicopter. We grabbed our signal flares and threw sea dye markers overboard. The helicopter flew directly to us and went into a noisy hover just a few feet above our heads. One by one, we abandoned our rafts and our party toys and swam to the rescue cable offered by the chopper. The rotating blades generated hurricane-like winds and waves that made swimming difficult. Individually, we caught the trailing cable, climbed into the attached harness and were hauled aboard the helo, dangling like fish on the line.

When you're in the water and that huge mass of metal in motion is directly above you, you just KNOW that it's going to fall on you and ruin your day. There are just too many moving parts on a helicopter to ever achieve a satisfactory level of reliability. But when you're in extremis, or simulating it in a raft somewhere in the Pacific Ocean, nothing beats the sight of a noisy helicopter coming to get you. I discovered much later, in Southeast Asia, how important the

Search and Rescue helicopters and their crews were to the physical and mental well-being of a pilot in harm's way. God bless you, guys!

Years after the water survival course, I was in a hotel room somewhere, watching a PBS documentary about sharks. Almost every variety of marine killer was represented in the show: great whites, tigers, makos, hammerheads, etc. As I watched that TV show, I thought back to that afternoon, once upon a time, when an extremely vulnerable group of pilots floated in rafts in the waters off of San Diego. I know that sharks were a topic of conversation back then and that we would have been nervously wary, but we never saw any evidence of them.

At the end of the thirty minute documentary, the credits started to roll across the screen. The very last entry lingered for what seemed to be a very long time: "Filmed in the waters off of San Diego".

◆   ◆   ◆

The Navy injected land survival training into my life at random times during my military career. In northern Florida we were taught to catch crabs and snakes; eating them was something I never mastered. In the Philippines, we learned jungle survival from the Negritos, a sturdy race of mountain people native to and comfortable with the tropical forest environment. In the Philippines, the snakes were large enough to eat us.

SERE School was a survival experience that all three branches of the military deemed necessary after studying the conduct of American prisoners of war in prior conflicts. Potential POW's, said the government, required survival training in the techniques of staying alive and resisting interrogation while being abused or tortured in an enemy prison camp. SERE School (Survival Evasion Resistance Escape) became a requirement for everyone flying over enemy territory, thereby becoming subject to the possibility of capture. Of all the survival schools that I endured, SERE School was the most distasteful, difficult and frightening.

The classroom portion of the course began on a Monday morning. By Wednesday we were hustled aboard buses that would take us into the mountains east of San Diego, somewhere in the vicinity of Warner Springs. We were dropped off at a central staging area and given the rules of the game. We were to consider ourselves downed airmen in a hostile country, subject to capture and imprisonment. A stash of food had been positioned some distance forward of our location. It was our mission to secure the food without being captured by the enemy patrols in the area. Since none of us had eaten since the night before, the food was inviting. But moving around in daylight, in enemy territory, was a major *faux pas*. "Never mind," said the instructors. "Get moving!"

Those pilots who set off at a dead run, with the food as destination, were the most successful. Those of us who cautiously moved through the underbrush, trying to avoid detection and capture, were caught just as surely as those who sprinted to the food stash. But the latter were better fed.

The prisoner of war experience began with our capture. Soldiers with realistic weapons, strange uniforms and foreign accents restrained us, strip searched us and reclassified us with individual numbers and titles. I was now "War Criminal # 84".

We were relocated to a barbed wire enclosure complete with guard towers, interrogation rooms and punishment cells. Over the course of the next four days, we were interrogated, beaten and abused. It was no longer a game. We thought of ourselves as prisoners and we came to hate our tormentors.

I managed to avoid some of the individual abuse because I refused to answer when the camp public address system summoned War Criminal # 84 to the interrogation room. At one point, however, I was grabbed from behind and thrown to the ground. The guard felt the improvised knife that I had smuggled in the collar of my shirt and dragged me to a series of wooden boxes that were just large enough to contain a man in the crouching position. I was forced into a box and the lid was slammed on top of me. Because I was slightly smaller than average, the miniature cell was not as confining as it could have been. Not terribly susceptible to claustrophobia, I squeezed my head down between my knees to take advantage of the breathing holes at the bottom of the box and tried to relax in the dark. Actually, it was the first time that anyone had left me alone in the past few days. I found the experience not unpleasant.

Another pilot, a full-sized guy, was shoved into the box next to me. I don't know what his crime was, but from the groans emanating from his private prison, I could hear that he wasn't enjoying himself. I listened to his discomfort for some time, then I heard the lid on his box open and slam shut again. Almost immediately, there was an inhuman cry and I heard the sound of splintering wood. I found out later that one of the guards had caught a rattlesnake, cut off its head and threw the body, still squirming, into the box with the other pilot. When he sensed that he wasn't alone in that tiny, dark, confined space, he fairly exploded out of it.

I was in the box for less than an hour. Then it was back to the prison experience: hours spent doing nothing in the southern California sun with a constant low-grade headache from lack of food. Once in a while, a prisoner would be singled out for harassment and then returned to the group. Day after day, we existed. We had minimal water and no food. An hour would feel like a day. A day was an eternity. The prison experience reinforced a concept that became inviolable: I was never, EVER going to be a POW!

One of the E-2 pilots was paraded before us. I knew him casually as a member of the electronic warfare squadron whose mission was to orbit the carrier, extending the range of the ship's radar umbrella. He had been interrogated and beaten. He stood in front of us, between two guards, whimpering and sobbing, dressed in the uniform of the guards. Whatever they did to him, it was more than he could bear. To end his suffering, he had accepted the carrot that the guards offered.

One of the guards grabbed another pilot prisoner who was sprawled on the ground near me. He stood him before the traitor and told him to punch the pilot in the stomach. He accomplished his task with enthusiasm. If the guards had told him to kill his fellow pilot, I'm sure that he would have complied. What a disgusting and demoralizing display of cowardice!

On Saturday night the guards summoned all of the prisoners to a public meeting. On a make-shift stage in front us, the senior officers of the group were humiliated. One commander, who was slotted to become the executive officer of an already deployed, operational squadron was knocked off the stage with such force that he broke his arm. Obviously, his XO billet would be filled by someone else. At that particular moment, I was grateful to be a lowly junior officer.

On Sunday morning, we were told that we were to be "repatriated." We were lined up and offered a foul smelling concoction, the first food since the previous Tuesday night. If we didn't eat it we were ordered to pour it over our heads. Pour it I did. My stomach had already shrunk to starvation size and I decided to wait for something better.

Shortly thereafter, we were herded into buses that would take us to the base at San Diego. I was given an orange. I couldn't finish it. Fifteen pounds lighter than when I started, I was finally free from the malevolent guards who had starved, beaten, interrogated and abused us. SERE School was the longest, most unpleasant week of my life. I never saw the cowardly E-2 pilot again but I'm quite confident that he was never sent to Vietnam. Maybe that was his intention.

Every naval training facility displays photographs of its instructors, with the name and rank of each teacher immediately below his photo. The SERE School also posted pictures of its instructors but without any name and rank identification. These guys could have come from any branch of service, if indeed they were in service at all. The one unifying characteristic that they shared was the look in their eyes. Their eyes were cruel.

Years later, I was visiting a man who lived in Fort Dodge, Iowa. A neighbor knocked at his back door and came into the kitchen where we were talking. When I glanced at the intruder's face, my heart stopped! I recognized the cruel eyes that I had known once upon a time. After he had gone, I inquired about him. "Oh, he works at the local slaughter house," I was told. "He kills the hogs."

7

Vertigo

Vertigo killed John F. Kennedy, Jr.

On Friday, July 16th, 1999, John Kennedy was piloting a single engine aircraft destined for the airport at Martha's Vineyard, an island off the coast of Massachusetts. Cruising above 10,000 feet over Long Island Sound as the sun was setting, his visibility would have been unrestricted by the haze and moisture below him and the horizon would have been clearly visible on his easterly heading. Behind him, the fading oranges and reds of the aging sunset lingered. As he descended for his approach and landing, the sky would have transitioned from a dusky sunset to a fuzzy darkness that refracted the high intensity strobe of his anti-collision light. The haze would have thickened and the horizon would have disappeared as he descended to a landing altitude of sixty-seven feet above sea level. Although the night visibility around the Martha's Vineyard Airport still met the criteria for Visual Flight Rules (a lighted object could be seen from a distance of three statute miles), the absence of the horizon and the lack of lighted objects in the blue-black ocean below his aircraft would have made piloting extremely difficult. Unless, of course, John Kennedy had been taught to ignore the normal sensations of his body and to rely exclusively on his flight instruments.

Vertigo is the disorienting phenomenon that convinces a pilot that his flight instruments are lying to him. It is only a problem when visual cues are unavailable….if a pilot can see for himself that the sky is above him and the ocean is below him, he knows that he is right side up. When the visual cues disappear, inertia, spatial confusion and the normal functioning of the fluid system of the inner ear combine to disorient and confuse a pilot. When flying straight and level over water on a dark, horizonless night, it is vertigo that convinces a pilot that he is upside down. To overcome it, he must first recognize it and then consciously choose to ignore the "seat of the pants" sensations that are confusing him. He must compel himself to trust his flight instruments. Vertigo is a formidable threat to aviators of all experience levels, but it is lethal to those who are ignorant of its perils.

In May of 1969, I was the newest pilot assigned to VA-93, a Navy A-7 Corsair squadron based in Lemoore, California. I was a replacement for someone who had been promoted, mustered out of the Navy or killed. VA-93 had recently completed a combat cruise in the western Pacific flying the A-4 Skyhawk, the Corsair's predecessor. The squadron was transitioning to the A-7 and was scheduled to return to Vietnam aboard the USS Ranger in six months. The training cycle was well under way when I arrived, but I was warmly welcomed and quickly accepted. I was a new and inexperienced pilot on his first cruise. In Navy parlance: a nugget.

At the end of June, the skipper of VA-93, Commander Tom Schaaf, proposed a recreational cross-country trip to Elmendorf Air Force Base at Anchorage, Alaska. The official purpose of the trip was training, but in reality, it was a boondoggle to load up on king crab. I jumped at the chance and found myself the most junior aviator of a group of four. We were to leave on the evening of June 30th, spend the night in Whidbey Island, Washington, and then enjoy a glorious day of aviation sight-seeing along the western shore of Canada, north to Alaska.

In June of 1969, the air traffic controllers were on strike. On the evening of the 30th, we waited for hours in hopes of obtaining an FAA clearance to fly at the efficient high altitude cruise levels of the upper atmosphere. It finally became obvious that because of the shortage of controllers, clearances were rationed and boondoggle Navy flights were low on the priority list. Eventually, Tom decided that we would fly below the air traffic control system airspace. He told us to man our airplanes.

Four A-7's taxied onto runway 32 Left at Lemoore Naval Air Station, two on the left side of the runway and two on the right side. I was the junior pilot in the formation so I was assigned to be the skipper's wingman, the number two position. Lieutenant Don Dill was number three, the leader of his two plane section. Commander Schaaf held up his right hand and rotated his index finger, signaling full power on the engines. Then, with a drop of that same hand, he signaled me to release the brakes on my aircraft and follow him into the air. The two of us simultaneously roared down the left half of the runway, accelerating rapidly past 150 miles per hour, and rotated into the evening sky. I transitioned to close formation, still on his right side, and raised my landing gear and flaps when he did. He was using a little less than full power on his engine to provide me a "catch-up cushion" to adjust my position relative to his aircraft.

Don Dill and his wingman took off thirty seconds after us. Soon, the four of us, in a comfortable cruise formation, climbed northwest above the San Joaquin Valley, enjoying the dusky, hazy sunset on our left side. Initially, we leveled at 18,500 feet. We didn't have a clearance to be in the Area of Positive Control which started at 24,000 feet but as long as we could operate in visual conditions, eighteen thousand feet would nicely clear any mountains in the area. I crossed beneath the skipper's aircraft from right to left and settled in to fly formation, unaware that somewhere below my seat a wire from the aircraft to the speakers in my helmet had flexed one too many times and had finally broken.

The top of the haze layer crept up to our altitude. Commander Schaaf added power and climbed. He leveled this time at 23,500 feet but we were still in the haze and by now, it was dark. The horizon to the west was no longer visible and Tom was flying and navigating strictly on instruments, almost certainly on his autopilot. I tucked my aircraft a little closer to his, using his airplane as my entire frame of reference. Wing tip to wing tip, there couldn't have been more than ten feet between us. If he'd been upside down, it wouldn't have mattered to me; I just concentrated on maintaining my relative position to his aircraft. Smooth and steady, Tom was an experienced flight leader who avoided any abrupt changes in heading or altitude that his wingmen would have difficulty following.

Don Dill and his wingman were on the skipper's right side, still flying a loose, comfortable formation. Probably too loose. I started sneaking a peak at Don's aircraft when I could because it seemed that the distance between his aircraft and the skipper's was changing, increasing and decreasing with random frequency. Don Dill was fighting vertigo and losing. He was too far from the skipper to pick up on small distance changes, too preoccupied with flying formation to rely on his own flight instruments and totally devoid of any external cues that might have helped him sort things out.

Tom Schaaf must have glanced in the rearview mirror mounted on the right upper edge of his canopy. He saw Don and his wingman barreling into him from behind and to his right. Instinctively, he reacted. He threw his aircraft into a sharp left turn, directly into my path. I yanked back on my controlstick to avoid Tom and pulled into a steep climb as the other three A-7's passed, just inches below me. I had a sensation of aircraft lights, diffused by fog, passing at high speed and very close.

I topped out somewhere around 30,000 feet as my aircraft completed the half-loop generated by my high-g panic pull on the controlstick. I rolled the airplane right-side-up and called to the others on the radio. No answer. I tried again and again. No answer. Four Corsairs had been flying in close proximity just moments ago. Now I felt very much alone, peering into the dark haze. "They're all dead," I thought.

I circled for a few minutes in the fog but I couldn't see a thing. Eventually, I turned to the southeast and tuned in an air traffic control frequency on my radio. I called Oakland Center. When they didn't reply, I tried a different frequency. Still no answer. By now I was beginning to doubt that my radio was working.

On the chance that my transmitter was working and my receiver was inoperative, I keyed the microphone switch on the throttle and briefly described the location of the possible mid-air collision. I told air traffic control, if they could hear me, that I was headed for Lemoore Naval Air Station.

I continued on my southeasterly heading, eventually flew out of the haze and the lights of the towns and the cities in the valley appeared below me. North of Sacramento, I saw the lights of Beale Air Force Base 20,000 feet below me. I dialed in the Beale tower radio frequency and told the tower that I was overhead, enroute to Lemoore.

"If you can hear me," I said, "turn your runway lights off and on."

Almost immediately, two miles of white lights on either side of Beale's runways blinked off and then on again. I wasn't alone.

A few miles north of Navy Lemoore, I noticed an aircraft's anti-collision lights in my rear view mirror. It was Commander Schaaf rapidly closing on me from behind. He had used air traffic control's radar to locate me and to make sure that his wingman was out of harm's way. Slowly and carefully, Tom closed the distance between us until he was tucked into a tight position on my left wing. He motioned for me to join up on him. I acknowledged with a salute and slid aft along his aircraft to resume the formation that we had begun earlier in the evening. As a flight of two A-7's, we landed and taxied to the squadron flight line.

Later, as we debriefed over a cup of coffee, Commander Schaaf explained that Lieutenant Dill had been temporarily disoriented by the hazy flight conditions and had misjudged the rate of closure within the formation. He thanked me for avoiding a potentially catastrophic mid-air collision. It was not my place to pursue the issue any further and nothing more was ever said about it. Don and his wingman, wiser airmen for their experience, were waiting for the skipper at Whidbey Island Naval Air Station. The skipper refueled, left me and my broken airplane and flew north to rejoin the rest of the formation.

Vertigo was a common nuisance to naval aviators because of night carrier operations. It was never pleasant or comfortable to make a low altitude approach to an aircraft carrier on a horizonless night when you just KNOW, when all of your bodily sensations are screaming, that you are upside down and about to fly into the water. But we recognized vertigo for what it was and forced ourselves to believe the information from our flight instruments. I wish that John Kennedy had done the same.

8

Vietnam

Rick Stephenson and I met our future brides during the months preceding the Ranger cruise. Rick, even more impetuous than I, married his California girl after a whirlwind courtship that couldn't have lasted more than a month. He had a few weeks of marital bliss, sans honeymoon; then he and I and the rest of the 4,500 members of the USS Ranger crew departed from the port of San Francisco on an all expense paid trip to Vietnam and other western Pacific garden spots.

Our first port of call was Hawaii. With the Ranger safely anchored in historic Pearl Harbor, and no scheduled flight operations, Rick and I went ashore to explore. One morning we rented a car and drove counterclockwise around the island of Oahu. We spent the day admiring deserted beaches and beautiful, tropical scenery. Late in the day, we returned the rental car and hiked the short distance to the Ranger's gangplank. Aboard the ship, we discovered that mail call had been generous and we retired to our respective staterooms to devour the letters from our ladies.

I didn't see Rick for some time after that, but his roommate took a few of the pilots aside and described the tragedy that had befallen him. The letter Rick had received from his wife was a "Dear John." She told him that she had removed all of his belongings from their apartment, taken a new lover and had filed for divorce. Rick was devastated.

When he was able to compose himself, Rick sat with Tom Schaaf, the commanding officer of our squadron, and explained his situation. Rick felt that if he could confront his wife face to face, he might be able to save his marriage. At worst, he would be able to reconcile himself to the situation. He requested a leave to return to California. The skipper refused, explaining that we were on a combat cruise and that everyone on board had very good reasons for wanting to return. He told him, however, that if he would turn in his Navy wings, he would send him home.

Like all of us, Rick had worked too hard for those wings and loved flying too much to turn his back on naval aviation. Over time, he came to understand that confronting his bride would not save his marriage. But that realization did little to ameliorate his pain.

After a week in port, the Ranger left Pearl to conduct flight operations in and around the waters of the Hawaiian Islands. Rick kept to himself most of the time but once in a while, I would see him as he forced himself to complete his assigned flights. The change in his appearance was dramatic. The broad-shouldered blonde athlete had been replaced with a sunken-eyed gaunt shadow of his former self. None of us knew what to say to him.

Weeks later, we were off the coast of South Vietnam in a carrier operating area known as Dixie Station. It was common for an air group to operate in the relatively low threat environment of Dixie Station for a few weeks to allow its pilots to get their swords bloody and their confidence up while working in a relatively low threat environment. We did some close air support for the Army and Marine troops in the jungle and dropped bombs on suspected areas of enemy infiltration. Any fire directed at us would have come from small arms (rifles, pistols or machine guns) and would not have represented much of a threat to a fast moving jet. Unless, of course, they happened to hit us.

A couple of weeks later, the Ranger steamed north to Yankee Station, a carrier operating area in the Tonkin Gulf off the coast of heavily defended North Vietnam. Our missions would shortly involve attacking targets in North Vietnam and Laos. Neither location would be easy or pleasant.

Two aircraft carriers were usually assigned to Yankee Station. In order to run flight operations twenty-four hours per day, the carriers would alternate operating periods from noon to midnight or from midnight to noon. Each pilot on the individual ships would fly two missions per day, one in daylight and one at night. At least that was the plan. If your ship happened to draw the midnight to noon schedule, it was not unusual to get stuck with mostly night missions.

Standard operating procedure required that an untested neophyte pilot be paired with an experienced leader for serious combat missions. So it was that Lieutenant Commander Dave Rogers and I sat down to brief my first mission. Dave was a veteran of several prior cruises, at least one of which had been in Southeast Asia. He discussed every aspect of our upcoming flight from the pre-flight inspection of our aircraft to the post flight debrief. In his low-keyed monotone he talked of radio frequencies, rendezvous procedures, target tactics, emergency considerations, fuel constraints and recovery/landing techniques. He insisted that we understand each other thoroughly and be able to work together efficiently as a team. The longer we talked, the higher my heart rose in my throat.

Finally, we had just enough time to take a nervous piss before climbing the ship's ladders to the flight deck for the launch.

The techniques for delivering a five hundred pound dumb (unguided) bomb to a target have evolved over generations of Navy pilots and scores of airplanes. The objective is to "pickle" the bomb off of the airplane with the appropriate velocity vector, allowing the laws of physics and ballistics to complete the bomb's journey from the airplane to its intended target. Weapons delivery techniques are also designed to permit the delivering aircraft to escape the bomb blast and to minimize the response of the defenders. I have yet to meet a fellow pilot who was fond of Kamikaze missions.

For months before the cruise, the squadron pilots refined their bombing skills on various ranges scattered throughout California and Nevada. The procedures became second nature and most of us felt as comfortable upside down in a steep dive as we did flying upright, straight and level.

The typical dive bomb attack began at 10,000 feet above ground. At that altitude, a pilot would orbit the target, visually maintaining it at the tip of one of his wings. To begin the dive, the pilot would roll toward the target until his aircraft was upside down. Then, maintaining a positive g-loading on the controlstick, he would pull the nose of the airplane down to the target, align the gun sight on it and roll the wings level and upright. If the maneuver were done properly, the aircraft would be upright, in a forty-five degree dive with the airspeed rapidly accelerating. At 5,000 feet above ground level, as the target was growing larger in his gun sight and his airspeed was approaching 520 miles per hour, he would punch the bomb release button on the controlstick, electrically disconnecting the bombs from the airplane, allowing them to begin their solo journeys. At that point, the pilot had one primary consideration: to get the hell out of there! Usually a 7-g pull-up was sufficient to get the airplane climbing again, but add a little adrenaline from a late pull-up point or a heavy dose of anti-aircraft artillery and it was possible to pull the wings right off of the airplane.

Lieutenant Commander Rogers and I joined up in a loose cruising formation after our respective catapult shots. We were both carrying ten Mark 82 500 pound bombs on the wing racks. We coasted into Vietnam just south of the Demilitarized Zone, separating the North from the South, at an altitude of 20,000 feet. What a beautiful country Vietnam is, at least from the air. White, pristine beaches line the coast for mile after mile. Green forests of impenetrable jungle carpet the ground as far as the eye can see. Except for the little hairs standing at attention at the back of my neck, we could have been on a scenic cross-country trip in a peaceful part of the world.

Somewhere over Laos, west of the DMZ, we rendezvoused with the Air Force forward air controller to whom we had been assigned. Flying a maneuverable OV-10 observation aircraft, he was very familiar with the country below. We traded some quick pleasantries over the radio and then he put us to work. Violently maneuvering his aircraft, he pointed his nose briefly at a grove of trees and fired a smoke rocket. Immediately, a burst of anti-aircraft artillery erupted from the trees, white-hot phosphorous tracers arching gracefully toward his aircraft. He deftly maneuvered away from the hot spot and then called us on the radio, instructing us to drop our bombs just a little to the northeast of the smoking rocket in the trees.

Dave Rogers acknowledged the FAC's directives and positioned his aircraft for the dive. A few seconds later, he called, "Raven one is in. Hot." I waited until he called "off target" to begin my first run. I flipped on the master arm switch and selected two bombs, one on each side of the aircraft. Then I rolled my aircraft inverted and into the target as I had practiced. As soon as I had rolled the wings level and was established in my dive, I saw the tracers zipping past my canopy. Someone on the ground was desperately trying to hit me before I released my bombs. At the pickle point, I hit the bomb button and began pulling out of the dive, simultaneously banking hard to the right to get away from the stream of white light tracking me. I banked back to the left as twin explosions rocked the jungle just short of where I was aiming. Whew! These gunners are playing for keeps and it looks like they'd had a lot of practice.

Dave and I made four more runs apiece and then bid *adieu* to the Air Force. As we crossed the coastline, enroute to the USS Ranger, I felt a great sense of relief to have water below me once more. My first real combat experience was behind me and I felt euphoric. As Winston Churchill once said, "There is nothing more exhilarating than to be fired upon without effect."

Eventually, we all settled into the tempo of the times and executed our daily missions as directed by the FAC *du jour*. Most of our missions were useless exercises in bombing trees. Once in a while, however, something interesting would happen.

There was an area in central Laos, along the Ho Chi Minh Trail, that was especially ugly. It was thick with anti-aircraft artillery and had claimed many Navy and Air Force casualties. It was an area that was notorious for the torture and summary execution of any airman unfortunate enough to be shot down within its confines. We decided to clean house.

A strike group of six A-6's, fourteen A-7's and four F-4's launched from the Ranger one winter afternoon. Our ordnance load was thousand pound bombs and CBU's. Cluster bomb units are canister-contained, hand grenade-sized explosives that disperse over a broad area when the main canister opens in flight. CBU's are especially effective against troops and unfortified gun positions. I was carrying thirteen CBU's myself, enough tiny bomblets to obliterate thirteen football fields.

Each flight was assigned a target within that unpleasant section of Laos. I rolled in on my objective and released all thirteen CBU canisters. Climbing off target, I looked over my shoulder at a fascinating demonstration. Tiny dust puffs, covering a wide area, were walking through the cratered countryside. Every fifty yards or so, a larger secondary explosion would occur as a gun emplacement detonated. That region of Laos was quiet for weeks.

The twin mountain passes where the Ho Chi Minh Trail left North Vietnam and entered Laos were also heavily defended and nasty. There was at least one nuisance surface-to-air missile (SAM) site located across the border from Laos that had been tracking strike aircraft working in the vicinity of the passes, triggering SAM warnings in the cockpits. So far, it had not fired any missiles.

VA-93 was tasked to send a couple of A-7's armed with radar-homing Shrike missiles to the Ban Kari and Mhu Gia Passes in an attempt to eliminate the threat before it became operational. Tom Anderson and I drew the mission.

Tom was a tall, blonde Swede who was also from Northern Illinois. He and I had flown from California to Navy Glenview, near Chicago, the previous summer on a cross country trip to visit our respective families. The day before we were scheduled to leave Illinois, I attended a family reunion. At the reunion, my brother-in-law, Maurice Foley, suggested that I fly over his company picnic on my return trip to California. It seemed like a marvelous idea.

Federal Aviation Regulations expressly forbid aircraft operating below 10,000 feet to exceed 250 knots or 287 miles per hour. But in 1969, that rule didn't really apply to military jets who could claim an operational need to fly faster. And in 1969, that speed limit was rarely enforced.

Two Navy Corsairs, in close formation, a thousand feet above the ground, roared over Maurice Foley's Sunday picnic at an airspeed approaching 450 miles per hour. Maurice told me later that the picnickers were momentarily stunned by the sight and the sound of the fast-moving jets. He delighted in explaining to everyone that the commotion was only his brother-in-law returning to his Navy base in California.

Tom and I orbited the SAM site. The countryside below was gorgeous. Limestone karsts projected hundreds of feet vertically out of lush, emerald green rain forests. It often occurred to me that this country, with its white sand pristine beaches, tropical climate and lush forests would make a wonderful vacation hide-away. Assuming, of course, that the inhabitants stop trying to kill each other.

I flipped the switch that supplied electrical power to the Shrike, turned on the master arm switch that controlled the entire aircraft weapons system and waited. Tom was off my right wing in a spread formation, watching for threats of any kind, allowing me to track the site. For about an hour we played cat and mouse. The SAM site would track us and prepare to fire a missile. I, in turn, would track the radar transmitter at the site, roll into a launch dive for the Shrike and move my finger to the trigger switch. Then, someone on the ground would reconsider his options and the entire site would shut down. I'd lose my tracking solution on the missile, pull out of my dive and return to the orbit. Finally, it was time to return to the ship. I deselected the master arm switch and set a course for the DMZ.

As we passed over the Demilitarized Zone on our way out to sea, a marine on the ground called us on the radio. He inquired whether we had any machine gun ammunition left. The A-7 has 2, twenty-millimeter cannons mounted in the nose that fire a 10 inch projectile with an explosive tip. Mounted basically just out-board of the pilot's feet, the guns generate a heavy duty vibration when they fire.

I told the marine that we were armed and asked him what he needed. He explained that he was observing enemy troops moving supplies across the border in wheel barrows. I asked him to mark the location. He fired a smoke grenade in the general vicinity of the wheel barrows and I rolled in on it. I flipped the master arm switch on, hit the toggle switch that arms the guns and felt the solid double thump below my feet as the heavy cannon breeches locked into place.

About three thousand feet above the ground, I squeezed the trigger and the guns fired. About a second later, I heard a massive WHOOSH and saw the smoke and flame of the Shrike missile accelerate past me. I pulled up and away from the target muttering "Oh, shit! The Shrike fired!" When Tom and I left the SAM orbit, I had turned off the master arm switch but had neglected to turn off the Shrike switch. When I armed the guns, the Shrike was already selected and ready. I just won the "dumbshit of the day award."

The marine was ecstatic.

"Do you have any more of those? That was great! You should see those guys run!"

Tom and I climbed back to altitude and headed for the ship. Now I would have the privilege of explaining why I fired a $100,000 missile at a wheel barrow.

◆   ◆   ◆

After flight operations were secured for the day, the ship's flight deck crew would routinely reposition the aircraft on deck and secure them with heavy chains. Then the tugs themselves would be secured and chained down. The ship would steam silently through the night in quiet contrast to the controlled and violent cacophony of the previous hours of flight operations.

One dark overcast night, a young man erupted onto the calm flight deck and ran screaming until he disappeared over the side, falling sixty feet to the inky, black water below. According to witnesses, he had yelled something about being unable to handle the stress. An emergency attempt to locate him in the water failed. An "all hands muster" was ordered by the commanding officer of the ship in an attempt to discover the identity of the missing man. The ship's laundry officer, a young ensign, was, indeed, missing. It's ironic that in the midst of a combat cruise, when so many of the ship's personnel were involved in arming, launching and flying dangerous machines, the ship's laundry created the first stress casualty.

On December 24, 1969, Bob Hope and Company arrived aboard the Ranger. Neil Armstrong, Connie Stevens, The Golddiggers (some of the best looking round-eyed women our home-sick sailors had seen in months), Teresa Graves, Miss World, Suzanne Charny, and Les Brown and his Band of Renown combined to produce a Christmas show in the hangar bay. For a few hours, we were home and the war was a distant memory. To this day, I can't hear the name Bob Hope without remembering, with gratitude, the man and his troupe for flying halfway around the world to bring Christmas cheer to the lonely sailors of the USS Ranger.

The show ended at 11:30 pm. The Ranger commenced flight ops at midnight.

As I preflighted my aircraft for that first launch, I noticed that the ordnance team had written "Merry Christmas" in green marker on my bombs. A cold chill ran up my spine. Never before had I felt such a strong premonition that this was to be my last day on earth. I went through the motions of preparing for engine start and launch, but I was overwhelmed by a sense of personal doom. There had been, by this time, many missions that I would have preferred to avoid but never before was I utterly convinced that I was about to die. I murmured a silent prayer and forced myself to concentrate on the pre-launch procedures. I tried to distance myself from the depression that was trying to envelope me.

In spite of my premonition, the entire flight was routine. It was the one and only time that I ever observed green tracers fired at us. Much later I discovered that Russian AK-47's frequently spew green tracers and that it wasn't a Christmas phenomenon.

A wise man once declared that courage is not the absence of fear. Courage is doing your duty in spite of fear. In retrospect, I'm glad that I completed that mission, if only for the wisdom that lingers. Christmas morning, 1969, became a low point in my life, something I would always remember and compare with future Christmases. Hey, stuck in Lincoln, Nebraska, and all alone on Christmas? That's not so bad. I remember a Christmas when someone shot at me with green tracers…

A few weeks after the holidays, Rick Stephenson met his fate. He had recovered somewhat from his wife's betrayal and was talking about beginning a new life after the cruise, maybe taking a motorcycle trip with Sonny Kifer. He never recovered the *joie de vivre* that he once exuded, but at least he appeared to be functioning again.

Perhaps he was distracted. Or maybe something failed mechanically in his aircraft. But Rick crashed into the night sea just a mile in front of the ship after a routine launch. His body was never recovered and his name is on the Vietnam Wall in Washington, D.C. His disloyal wife, now officially his widow, collected his $10,000 GI death benefit and requested all of his personal effects.

◆   ◆   ◆

One of the most satisfying personal memories of my military years occurred during a Rest and Recreation (R & R) visit in Hong Kong. I was killing time in a bar near one of the terminals of the Star Ferry, the ubiquitous, cheap transportation that runs between the island of Hong Kong and the mainland city of Kowloon. At the time, I was wearing the khaki aviation uniform of the brown shoe Navy. (The black shoe Navy is that group of unfortunate souls who are relegated to ship board duty and have no connection to aviation. Like laundry officers.)

Seated on a bar stool to my left, with an empty seat between us, was a Marine sergeant, also on R&R. He noticed my wings and asked me what aircraft I flew. When I told him A-7's, he reached across the empty stool and shook my hand with a surprising amount of warmth and gusto. When I asked him why he was so enthusiastic, he told me his story. Once upon a time, he and his buddies were badly pinned down and in danger of being overrun somewhere in the jungles of

South Vietnam. A couple of Navy A-7's showed up and saved their day. He vowed that he would shake the hand of the first A-7 pilot that he met. I was that lucky man…

9

Sonny

Sonny Kifer was the best natural athlete I ever knew. My earliest recollection of him was during my final week of Aviation Officer Candidate School in Pensacola. One class ahead of him, I was the cadet officer assigned to supervise his battalion. In reality, I was the lackey of the Marine drill instructor who was really in charge, but I did have a small role in motivating and organizing the Saturday athletic competitions between officer candidate battalions.

One of the events in that weekly contest was the running of the obstacle course. Laid out completely in loose sand, the obstacles included twelve foot walls, hanging ladders and assorted other challenging devices. It was run at a full sprint from start to finish. Typically, a cadet in good physical condition would run the course in about two and a half minutes but it wasn't unusual to see that same cadet vomit his breakfast afterwards. Running in loose, dry sand demands incredible effort.

When Sonny ran the "O" course, he didn't appear to be exerting himself. He had such ease of motion, such athletic grace that he moved from one obstacle to the next with a smooth, economical rhythm. He would sprint past the finish line a full thirty seconds faster than everyone else, without the obligatory vomiting afterwards.

I lost track of Sonny after we received our commissions. He went through primary and advanced jet training, as I did, but he was sent to an east coast A-7 squadron. He was planning to make his deployments to the Mediterranean, not the western Pacific. The needs of the service changed that and Lieutenant Kifer was transferred to VA-93 to be included in the training cycle preceding our deployment to Vietnam.

Sonny and his roommate, Rick Stephenson, lived in the same apartment complex that I did in Lemoore and we saw each other often. Sonny's dark, good looks and southern drawl and Rick's tall, clean-cut athleticism were natural chick magnets. I observed many very attractive women coming and going from their apartment down the way.

As the date for our first deployment to Vietnam approached, our squadron spent more and more time aboard the USS Ranger practicing day and night carrier landings and strike missions with live and practice ammunition. Sonny and I decided to be roommates for the cruise and were assigned a two-man stateroom adjacent to the officer's wardroom. The wardroom cockroaches freely visited our accommodations whenever they felt unwelcome somewhere else. Our stateroom was the size of a small bedroom but with bunk beds and a tiny desk, we had adequate space for two pilots.

Sonny was from a small town in Louisiana and he loved his name. He used to brag that if you sent him mail addressed: Sonny, Newellton, Louisiana, it would arrive in his mail box. With his southern twang and his easy going ways, it was impossible not to like him. He did see the world a little differently from the rest of us, however, and when he said something kind of wacko in his Louisiana drawl, we just had to write it down. Thus the "Kifer Log" was created, the complete and unabridged sayings of Nathan O. "Sonny" Kifer aboard the USS Ranger and later, the USS Midway.

Just an example...A few of the pilots were standing around in the squadron ready room one afternoon. One of the larger guys who was anxious about his expanding waistline was discussing a new diet-exercise program. He was saying, "If someone walks eight miles a day, he could eat anything he wants."

Sonny entered the ready room just in time to hear that last sentence.

"Frick!" he said. "I could walk twenty miles and I still couldn't eat 'sparugus." It made the Kifer Log.

Sonny didn't smoke, drink alcohol or cuss. "Frick" was the worst word that ever came out of his mouth.

That first Ranger cruise lasted nine months. Sonny and I were never allowed to lead any of the combat missions over North Vietnam, South Vietnam or Laos. As first-tour pilots, we were always relegated to flying wing for one of the senior pilots in the squadron. On the second cruise, aboard the USS Midway, we planned and led some of the strikes and, once in a while, we even flew a couple of missions together.

The Midway was an interesting ship. Constructed in 1945 and modernized in 1970, it heaved like all aircraft carriers do. In other words, as it moved through the sea swells, its flight deck would travel up and down vertically, providing a moving target for the pilots during approach and landing. The Midway's modernization program added a considerable amount of bulk steel and associated weight outboard of the island that towers over the flight deck. The net effect of the extra weight made the ship, and the flight deck, wallow as well as heave. Midway pilots had the distinct pleasure of watching the flight deck move in a horizontal figure eight pattern, even in calm seas. Stormy seas were even more volatile.

One night, Sonny and I were scheduled to fly together. We briefed the usual scenario in the ready room about an hour before launch, took one last nervous bathroom call and then suited up for the mission. In addition to the Navy-issue survival gear, I carried an H & K .22 caliber nine shot revolver loaded with hollow point ammunition. It was quieter and lighter than the standard .38 and much more accurate. With spare ammunition, survival radios and knife, I probably weighed thirty pounds more than normal.

About 30 minutes before launch time we were sitting in our cockpits awaiting the signal to "Start Engines." When it came, we started the big TF-41 turbofan engines and taxied toward the catapults. Sonny was on the port cat and I was on the starboard. Each of our A-7's was loaded with ten, MK-82, 500 pound bombs.

Following the directions of the deck crew, I lowered the launch bar attached to the nose wheel assembly and taxied forward until I felt the heavy thump as it locked into the catapult mechanism. The deck crew raised the blast deflector directly behind my aircraft; the catapult officer signaled me to release the brakes and to increase the engine to full power. The aircraft was now in the grip of the powerful steam catapult and would not move until the cat fired. I advanced the throttle with my left hand and locked my fingers around the T-handle just forward of the throttle mechanism, the throttle held firmly by the palm of my hand. The purpose of the T-handle was to provide an anchor for my throttle hand during the catapult acceleration. The force of the cat shot (and the inherent inertia of the throttle lever) is sufficient to retard the throttle during the violent two second acceleration of the aircraft. More than one naval aviator has gone for an unexpected swim for lack of a stiff throttle arm.

None of us enjoyed night catapult shots. A night take-off on a long runway allows the pilot to make a smooth, gradual transition to flight. A cat shot is just the opposite: one moment you're stationary on deck; the next, you're slightly discombobulated, low and slow, not absolutely certain whether you're climbing or on a ballistic trajectory headed for the water. We often quoted a pithy, Navy truism: "There never was a night cat shot that couldn't have prevented by a more thorough preflight." In other words, if you could find something mechanically wrong with your airplane, you could cancel the flight and go back to bed. A few pilots became notorious for refusing night missions but they were a small minority and their reputations suffered.

I stole a quick glance at the engine instruments, placed my head firmly against the headrest of the ejection seat, flipped the switch that turned on the exterior aircraft lights indicating that I was ready for launch, put my right hand behind the controlstick and waited…BAM! The catapult fired with a whoosh, my peripheral vision tunneled to a small fraction of normal from the transverse g-forces and the controlstick drifted back into my waiting hand. The 38,000 pound airplane accelerated from zero to almost two hundred miles per hour in about 1.5 seconds. I was flying, but just barely. Sixty feet above the night sea, the horizon nowhere in sight and my aircraft struggling slightly above stall speed, there was no margin for error.

Sonny launched a few seconds behind me, pointed his nose at my navigation lights and slowly joined up in formation. We headed west toward the land mass of Vietnam and a killing zone that had been expanding for a decade.

Our night missions were similar to our day tree-bombing exercises. Usually we would work with an Air Force FAC on targets of his choosing. On occasion, however, we would cruise the Ho Chi Minh Trail searching for targets of opportunity. In that scenario, one Corsair would fly 5000 feet above the network of roads, jinking back and forth, looking for military vehicles on the move. If he saw something suspicious, he would eject a parachute flare from a pod carried under his wing. When the flare ignited, it would illuminate a circular section of road almost a mile across. Any vehicles caught under the flare would have to scurry for cover in the artificial daylight, a sight reminiscent of cockroaches fleeing the sudden illumination of a darkened room. Another Corsair, paralleling his low wingman but flying at an altitude of 10,000 feet, would be in position to roll in on any trucks or convoys panicked by the flare.

One evening, I dove on a trapped convoy and became a target myself. I released four, 500 pound bombs at an altitude above a hanging flare, but all of the bombs came off the same side of my airplane. The imbalance flipped me upside down. My downward momentum carried me below the flare, illuminating a flailing, out of control A-7 to all of the local gunners within range. The resulting concentration of fire produced an adrenaline rush that helped me right my aircraft and escape to the safety of a higher altitude.

As Sonny and I cruised to our target area, we could see streams of tracers erupt at locations all around us but well below us. Sometimes a solitary gun would pump a few short bursts into the night sky. Once in a while we would witness four or five anti-aircraft guns shooting steady streams of intersecting tracers at an invisible intruder. From 25,000 feet above the jungle, our field of view encompassed a thousand square miles. In a perverse way, the scattered firefights in the jungle below reminded me of 4th of July celebrations in a country far away.

Sonny once told me a story about a novel targeting plan. He was flying with one of the crazier pilots in the squadron on a typical night mission. When their FAC didn't meet them at the assigned location, they were forced to dispose of 10,000 pounds of excess ordnance. Gaylord coaxed Sonny into making a mock bombing run with his navigation and anti-collision lights on in an area known to be heavily infested with anti-aircraft guns. When the gunners opened up on Sonny, Gaylord dropped all of his bombs on them. Then he flipped his lights on and made another run so that Sonny could return the favor.

This night, Sonny and I rendezvoused with an Air Force FAC, dropped our ordnance where he recommended, did little damage to the native jungle and departed his area. Our mission complete, I joined up on Sonny's aircraft for the return trip. In close formation, we took turns inspecting each other's airplane for any bullet holes or flak damage and then set a course over the DMZ and back to the Midway.

Throughout the flight, from launch to target, a solitary thought nagged at me. I dreaded the knowledge that all too soon I would be aiming my aircraft (and my own rear end) at the dark, heaving flight deck of the USS Midway. Another favorite naval quotation summed up the sentiment: practicing night carrier landings is like practicing bleeding! Landing aboard ship in the daytime is fun, but night operations *always* generate panic.

It was raining by the time we returned to the ship. To make matters worse, Sonny and I were to be the first aircraft recovered. At the moment, we were flying around the thunderheads in bright starlight. Underneath the overcast, steaming through the inky darkness of the night ocean, the undulating back end of the USS Midway waited.

I split off from Sonny and entered the marshal pattern at my assigned altitude. Each pilot is given a specific altitude and time to start his approach to the ship. By adhering to those times and flying identical inbound speeds from a common starting point behind the ship, the entire arrival can be conducted with minimal radio traffic. It is *imperative* that each pilot begin his approach from the assigned point at his designated time and fly the appropriate speed to the ship. About six miles from touchdown, the Midway's final radar controller assumes control of the aircraft and starts talking non-stop to the pilot, verbalizing glide slope and line-up deviations.

The intensity of the rain increased as I descended to the glide slope intercept altitude. There was nothing to see outside the windows so I concentrated on flying my instruments. My landing gear, flaps, slats and tail hook were all down. My airspeed had slowed to 140 miles per hour but the rain was making such a racket on the windshield that I had to turn up the radio volume to hear the controller's voice. I was about 800 feet above the water, descending on the verbal glide path provided by the reassuring voice in my headset. Three quarters of a mile from the ship, the voice told me: "Call the ball!"

I squinted through the dark and the rain to see the familiar green "meatball" centered between the amber horizontal datum lights of the Fresnel lens, the ship's optical glide slope. By maintaining that green "ball" just where it was between those amber lights, I should be able to fly right down to the deck, using peripheral vision for lateral line-up.

I touched down hard on the wet deck, my heart beating furiously. My hook grabbed a wire and I skidded to a stop. Now for the fun part! The arresting cable retracted slightly, just enough to provide a little slack, and the first of many taxi directors gave me the "hook up" signal. I raised the hook and taxied forward, away from the cables. I reached down, unlocked the wings and hydraulically folded them.

As I slowly taxied along the darkened carrier deck I was directed by a succession of helmeted young men with yellow extensions on their flashlights. There were no deck lights and policy forbad using aircraft taxi lights. The further forward on the deck that I traveled, the more difficult it was to see where the deck ended and the sixty foot drop to the water began. My safety was completely in the hands of the young men with the wands.

Because I was the first aircraft to land, I taxied fully forward along the starboard side of the deck, my right wheel just inches from the edge. My full attention was riveted on the waving yellow wands. The taxi directors were forbidden to move while they had control of an aircraft for fear of generating optical illusions in the cockpit. Each director would control an airplane for a limited amount of deck space and then pass the aircraft to the next director further down the deck.

I approached the bow and continued until the nose of the aircraft projected into the black nothingness over the water. Only then did the director signal a hard left turn and a full stop. Space is limited aboard ship and every inch is eventually crammed with parked airplanes. Parking in that number one spot on the bow, however, was my least favorite after-landing activity.

The men who worked the flight deck were marvelous choreographers. Exposed to the weather, the deafening noise and the controlled violence of departing and arriving monsters spewing flame and jet blast, these kids kept their cool. Once in a while an arresting cable would break, slashing across the deck, bisecting anyone unlucky enough to be in its path.

There was a mutual respect between the pilots and the deck crews. One night, I was leaving my parked aircraft and walking down the deck toward the ready room. Jet blast from an aircraft making a hard turn on the bow caught me and knocked me off my feet. I skidded down the deck toward the rotating propellers of a just-landed E-2 early warning aircraft. Instantly, three flight deck sailors dove on me and halted my progress, preventing decapitation.

As I climbed out of my aircraft this night, I could see that Sonny had parked in the bow spot just across from me on the port side. We walked to the ready room together, a good end to an interesting night. When we came to a place where we could hear each other, he summed up the evening.

"Frick," he said. "If my momma knew I was doing this, she'd be worried."

It made the Kifer Log.

10

The Rescue

A grand tradition of the Cold War demanded that whenever an American aircraft carrier steamed across the Pacific enroute to Vietnam, a Russian long range bomber would intercept it, sometimes even flying alongside the ship at low altitude. It was the Russians' way of letting us know that they knew we were there. A carrier would anticipate, of course, that the Russians were coming and would maintain a pair of F-4 Phantoms on 15 minute alert to intercept any inbound aircraft. If the Russians were to arrive unannounced and unescorted, the ship would be embarrassed, appearing complacent and vulnerable.

In the spring of 1971, the USS Midway was steaming westbound from Hawaii to Yankee Station and Vietnam. Somewhere in the middle of the Pacific Ocean the ship's radar detected a lone aircraft closing on the carrier. An alarm sounded and the ship turned into the wind to launch the fighter-interceptors. Those of us with no part to play in the ensuing drama positioned ourselves along the catwalks of the upper decks of the ship, hoping to get a look at the Russian Bear when it appeared.

Eventually, the Phantoms radioed the Midway that the unidentified aircraft was a Pan American 747, probably returning to San Francisco from Hong Kong. The Russians would come another day.

The next morning I was sitting in the squadron ready room skimming some of the overnight teletype messages when a couple of the F-4 pilots walked in. They were looking for an A-7 pilot to serve as a practice target for their radar intercepts. The Midway was going to take a break from its relentless westward journey and conduct flight operations for a few hours later that afternoon. Apparently, the ship wanted to make sure that the flight operations department was still sharp since no aircraft had been launched or recovered since we left Hawaii.

I quickly volunteered to be their bogey, their practice Russian intruder. I sat down with the F-4 pilots and listened as they briefed the flight. The plan was for the ship to launch two F-4's and one A-7, send us in opposite directions for about fifty miles and then turn us towards each other. The Phantoms would be using their target acquisition radars to locate and intercept me before I could fly over the ship. The entire exercise would be under the control of the Midway's radar controllers. It sounded like a marvelous way to get off of the ship for a time, get above the overcast and alleviate the boredom.

Later that afternoon, I taxied my Corsair onto the bow catapult, brought the engine to full power, checked over the engine and flight instruments and saluted the Catapult Officer, signaling that I was ready for launch. The cat fired and I was airborne, free of the monotonous life aboard ship for as long as my fuel would endure.

I retracted my landing gear and flaps and accelerated to climb speed. There were no bombs hanging under my wings this day and my Corsair was relatively light. My wing tanks held about four hours of fuel. As that fuel burned off, my aircraft would get even lighter and more maneuverable.

I selected one of the tactical channels on my communication radio and checked in with the Midway's radar controller. He assigned me a heading to fly. In a moment I heard the F-4's call airborne on the same radio frequency. They were given the reciprocal heading from mine for their climb course and the distance between the three aircraft rapidly increased.

Somewhere around 9,000 feet I popped out of the overcast into bright, blue skies. It was glorious! After being cooped up on that slow-moving gray ship for a week, here I was, free as a bird, climbing and rolling in God's beautiful sunshine, a white carpet of clouds at my feet. In the middle of the Pacific Ocean there was no dust or haze to restrict the visibility. I could see forever!

It was unusual to be flying without a wingman but that only added to the exhilarating sense of freedom. I was supposed to be a challenge for the Phantoms: my single aircraft would be a very small radar target. If they could locate and intercept me, the much larger Russian Bear should be easy. I decided to give them a run for their money.

I stopped climbing and eased back into the overcast. By skimming the tops of the clouds, I had an unrestricted view of the sky above me and I would be invisible to anyone searching from above or below. And the sense of speed was incredible as I zipped through the tops of the white, puffy stratocumulus clouds.

Five minutes had elapsed when the radar controller told us to reverse course. The game was on! I threw my aircraft into a sixty degree left bank and maintained my altitude. I rolled out on the reciprocal heading from the original course and began scanning the sky above me.

The controller was giving the F-4's continuous bearing and distance to my aircraft as we closed on each other. By inverting the bearing information they were getting, I could tell what sector of the sky they were coming from. With about twelve miles between us, I saw them. They were 10,000 feet above me, in an abeam formation, about 1,000 feet apart.

I added full power to the engine and let the airspeed build to 480 miles per hour as I maintained my camouflage position in the cloud tops. The controller was telling the Phantoms that the distance between us was down to six miles. They still couldn't locate me. Apparently their radars were confusing my small target with normal ground clutter.

As they approached a position almost directly overhead, I banked hard to the left and began a steep climb toward them. I was climbing like a home-sick angel, closing the distance rapidly. By approaching the fighters from their left side and from below, and by maintaining a constant bearing to them, there was no relative motion for their eyes to react to. The controller continued to provide bearing and decreasing distance to the Phantoms but they maintained their formation and gave no indication that they saw me as I flew closer and closer. Finally, the controller reported that all three aircraft were "merged blips" on his radar screen. The pilot in the number two F-4 looked to his left and saw me flying close formation with him. He acknowledged to the controller that he finally had me in sight. The tone of his voice betrayed his disgust with their performance. Fighters are supposed to be behind their intended quarry, not in front of it.

The controller split us up and we flew in opposite directions. Once more, I descended to the cloud tops. The course reversal and the eventual intercept were identical to the first time and when the controller called "merged blips," I was again flying wing on the number two Phantom.

I didn't know what the radar controller could visualize from his position in the bowels of the ship, but I was enjoying myself. The fighters, on the other hand, were upset. They declared the exercise complete and we returned to the ship. I wasn't invited to their debrief and they never asked me how I penetrated their defenses. In fact, they weren't interested in talking to me at all. But I had a good yuck at their expense and it did provide welcome relief from the tedium of sailing. If the Russians ever did show, they must have come across at high altitude because I never saw them. Maybe the fighters didn't either.

The Midway must have been ahead of schedule on its trek across the Pacific because the next day we were told that the ship would take another day off from steaming to conduct flight operations. What luck! I'd be able to escape the confining gray bulk of the ship for two days in a row.

The squadron scheduling officer assigned me an afternoon flight. My wing-man and I enjoyed an hour above the clouds performing rolls and loops and other high speed maneuvers. In the middle of the Pacific Ocean, hundreds of miles from land in any direction, the airspace is unregulated and uninhabited, and we took full advantage of it. Eventually, we returned to the ship, expecting a normal daytime approach and landing.

Daylight carrier landings are fun. When the ship is ready to recover aircraft and is steaming steadily into the wind, a formation of jets will approach from about five miles behind it, flying in close formation at an altitude of 800 feet and a speed of 400 miles per hour. The lead aircraft would be on the left of the forma-tion and all of the wingmen would be in echelon to his right. As the first aircraft in the formation passes abeam the starboard bow of the ship, he would throw his aircraft into ninety degrees of left bank and pull hard on the controlstick, main-taining his altitude and bleeding off his airspeed. At ten second intervals, each pilot in the formation would replicate the leader's maneuver. As each aircraft slowed and turned, it would drop its landing gear and flaps, decelerating to an airspeed computed by an angle of attack gauge in the cockpit. Eventually, each pilot would intercept the visual glide slope projecting from the rear of the flight deck, descending on that glide slope to a solid touchdown among the four arrest-ing cables in the landing area. The aircraft would then taxi out of the landing area just in time for the next airplane to arrive. It was an efficient way to recover a large number of airplanes in a very short time. But it worked only in the daytime. And only in good weather.

When we checked in with the Midway's radar controller he told us that a fog bank was obscuring the visibility and that we would not be using day visual recovery procedures. Each aircraft would fly an individual carrier controlled approach (CCA) to the ship just as we normally did for night operations. The controller ordered all of the aircraft to land with the taxi light illuminated. Taxi light on in the daytime? THAT was strange. The taxi light was a powerful lamp mounted on the nose of the A-7 that could illuminate hundreds of feet of con-crete ahead of the aircraft. We seldom used it at night…and never in the daytime.

A few minutes later I was following the instructions of the CCA final control-ler as I descended on the glide slope toward the ship. My landing gear, arresting hook and flaps were all down and my taxi light was on. The light was a mystery that tugged at my mind whenever I found an idle moment. The controller "talked" me to a point three quarters of a mile behind the ship and 300 feet above the water. Then he told me: "Call the ball!"

I looked up from my instruments, expecting to see the bright orange neon "meatball" of the Fresnel landing system on the rear end of the Midway. All I saw was fog. I knew that I was closing on the ship at 130 miles per hour from less than three quarters of a mile away but I couldn't see a thing! The landing signal officer, standing on a platform on the stern of the ship, could see my taxi light through the fog.

"Power!" he radioed and I jammed the throttle forward just a little.

"Come right!"

I banked to the right just slightly and immediately leveled my wings.

My wheels hit the deck and I instinctively went to full power on the engine just in case my arresting hook didn't snag a cable. There I sat for a long moment, engine roaring, restrained by my hook and the ship's cable, trying to sort out where I was and how I got there. Finally, the air boss radioed from his perch above the flight deck.

"It's OK, Roger. You're on deck. You can reduce the power."

I chopped the throttle, raised my hook and taxied out of the arresting gear, following the signals of the young director in front of me. I was still a bit stunned.

Everyone who was airborne with me must have made the same zero visibility approach and landing that I did, aided at the last moment by the landing signal officer's view of his taxi light. It was a good thing that that light worked…there wasn't anywhere else to land within a thousand miles.

◆   ◆   ◆

Within a couple of weeks we were settled into the routine of flying off Yankee Station in the Tonkin Gulf. Our missions normally took us to central Laos where we worked with Air Force forward air controllers (FACs), bombing trees. What a waste! Years later I would meet a pilot who survived the Battle of Britain. I listened to his stories and then I complained about my war.

"I never fired a shot or dropped a bomb in anger," I said. "And I certainly never had the feeling that I was defending my country from invasion from a foreign aggressor. All we did, on a day to day basis, was try to stay alive."

"Hey, don't kid yourself, Laddie," he said. "That's all we were trying to do, too. Just stay alive."

One morning, I was flying with one of my favorite people, Rudy Kohn, the commanding officer of VA-93. We arrived over a dense section of Laotian jungle. The FAC *du jour* insisted that it showed signs of being a massive truck park and supply depot on the Ho Chi Minh Trail. We had heard that story before. But we settled into an orbit around the target in preparation for dropping some 500 pound bombs to probe the area.

Rudy made the first run. As soon as he pointed his nose at the target and began his bombing run, the jungle erupted with 23-millimeter anti-aircraft fire from about four different sites. White hot tracers snaked up towards his airplane. He dropped two bombs right in the middle of the densely forested area, triggering a massive explosion. It was my turn.

I rolled my aircraft inverted and pulled the nose down, aiming the bomb sight just adjacent to the area Rudy had destroyed. Established in a forty-five degree dive, I rolled my wings level and tracked the target. Tracers zipped past my canopy as the gunners on the ground tried desperately to hit me before I released my bombs. 5,000 feet above the trees, I hit the bomb-release button on the control-stick and began a seven g pull-up, breaking off to the right of the target and away from the tracers. Again, the jungle erupted with massive explosions. There really was something in those trees.

Rudy and I each made four more runs, dropping a pair of bombs each time. By now, a section of the jungle the size of a small city was ablaze but the gunners continued to fire at us. Out of time and ordnance, we inspected each other's aircraft for battle damage and then rolled out on a heading that would take us back to the ship. The FAC thanked us for our efforts and spent the rest of the day working other strike aircraft on his target.

As luck would have it, Rudy and I returned to that same target later that night. By now the perimeter of the fire was three times as large as we had remembered, but the devastated area was totally peaceful. Not a soul took a shot at us while we probed and dove over the desolation outlined by the burning trees. Just a few hours earlier there had been people down there, enemy people, I suppose, but living, breathing fellow inhabitants of our planet who no longer existed. Eerily, I was struck with a poignant sadness, imagining the destruction and loss of life on the ground. The memory of that night haunts me still.

A few days later, Rudy and I were sitting in our aircraft, engines running, parked alongside each other on the flight deck of the USS Midway. While we waited for the beginning of the launch process, maintenance and ordnance personnel scrutinized our airplanes, looking for any fuel or hydraulic fluid leaks. A squadron maintenance chief slowly approached the right side of Rudy's airplane, just below the cockpit. He had noticed something that didn't look quite right and he wanted a closer look. I could see Rudy. His canopy was open and he was waving furiously at the chief below him, but because of the tremendous noise on the flight deck, he couldn't get his attention. The chief walked up to the airplane, ran his finger through some liquid that was escaping from a small hole below the cockpit and brought his finger to his nose to determine what kind of fluid it was. Only then did he take a step backwards to see Commander Kohn's pained expression.

The A-7 has a "relief tube" mounted in the floor of the cockpit. Rudy had forgotten to take a nervous piss before manning his airplane and he thought that he could get the job done while we waited for launch. The chief just smiled and went on about his business, equipped with another colorful story about his boss.

Later, as we made our way across the DMZ and into Laos, we were told that an Air Force F-4 had been shot down in the Ban Krai Pass on the border between North Vietnam and Laos. A rescue operation was underway and we were ordered to assist.

Depending on the location of a downed pilot, an assortment of rescue resources was available. If the airman was in a relatively low threat area, a Marine, Navy or Air Force helicopter could quickly find and extract him with very little outside assistance. If the downed aviator was in the vicinity of enemy troops and heavy equipment, or worse, anti-aircraft artillery, the situation was infinitely more dangerous. In the latter case, the troops, tanks and anti-aircraft fire would have to be eliminated or suppressed before a slow-moving helicopter could attempt a rescue. As combat pilots, we were grateful for one simple truth: the military did its best to take care of its own. If the search and rescue folks could get us out, they would bring us home. Some of the bravest people I've ever known were flying some of the slowest aircraft over the jungles of Southeast Asia.

The Ban Krai Pass was one of the nastiest areas of the Ho Chi Minh Trail. It was heavily defended by anti-aircraft guns in well-fortified positions, some of which were mounted on the six hundred foot limestone karsts that erupted in vertical columns from the jungle floor. This was going to be a difficult rescue.

Rudy checked in with the on-site commander. He told us that they had located the two crew members on the ground and that at least one of them was still alive. He assigned us a cluster of anti-aircraft guns on the northern fringe of the rescue area. Rudy and I each made two passes, dropping five, 500 pound bombs per run. What a hornet's nest! I had never seen such a concentrated barrage of enemy fire streaking toward my aircraft as I made my dives.

Out of ordnance, we wished the commander well and departed the area. Other Navy and Air Force strike aircraft were steadily arriving and being put to use against additional gun sites. The drama was far from over.

A few days later a contingent of Air Force pilots choppered out to the Midway. They were the on-site commanders who had coordinated the rescue in the Ban Krai Pass. They wanted to meet and thank the Navy pilots who had provided assistance and to let us know the outcome of the effort. This is their story:

After hours of non-stop strikes against the Ban Krai anti-aircraft guns, the Air Force Sandys arrived to provide close air support for the Jolly Green Giant rescue helicopters. The Sandys were vintage A-1 propeller aircraft that were armed with rockets and machine guns. They were no match for anti-aircraft guns, but they could eliminate enemy troops or at least keep them from bringing effective fire against the large, green, vulnerable helicopters.

The lead Jolly Green helicopter quickly located one of the downed Air Force F-4 pilots, confirmed his identity on his survival radio, swooped into a hover directly over his position in the jungle, sent down a jungle penetrator rescue seat and hauled him into the helo.

The other Jolly Green went after the second pilot, whose radio was broadcasting a locator signal only. On the assumption that he was injured and unable to respond, the helicopter hovered over his probable location and lowered a crewman on a rescue seat into the jungle canopy. As soon as the crewman broke through the trees, he saw the pilot. He was hanging in his parachute harness suspended above the jungle floor, either dead or unconscious, with his helmeted head dangling at an odd angle. It appeared that his neck was broken. The crewman clawed his way through the branches to the pilot and began to cut him free.

By now, the Jolly Green, a huge stationary target, was taking devastatingly accurate fire. The helicopter pilot made the only decision that could have saved his crew and his aircraft. The crewman in the jungle was hauled aboard and the chopper beat a hasty retreat. The other pilot was never recovered but the airman who came so close to retrieving him lapsed into a temporary state of shock. His adrenalin had been pumping so furiously and he was so totally focused on the rescue that when it failed by inches, his body shut down. He sat on the floor of the exiting helicopter, eyes open but unseeing. Eventually, after his excess adrenaline had dissipated, he resumed his station aboard the chopper, but in a state of total exhaustion.

The rescue helicopters and their fighter-escorts returned to their bases in Thailand and Laos with the lone survivor aboard. Hundreds of tons of ordnance had been dropped by the Navy and Air Force pilots in their rescue efforts. They had assumed great personal risk to save a comrade.

After the briefing, when the Air Force pilots had returned to their base, I was thinking about a crack that Bob Hope made aboard the USS Ranger during his

Christmas show in 1969. He was referring to the fact that so few of the ship's personnel actually participated in the war. "It must be terrible to wake up every morning and read about the war in the newspaper," he said. It produced a guffaw from the hundreds of officers and sailors in the audience.

Bob Hope was right on. Only a few of us on the USS Midway actually fought the war. But that is the way that air warfare has always been conducted. A large support team maintains, fuels and arms a warplane. Then a pilot and sometimes a couple other crewmembers take that plane into battle. It's an exclusive fraternity of air warriors who willingly risk their lives to fly the missions or save a comrade. It's rare that someone outside of the fraternity appreciates or understands.

One night I landed on the Midway, parked on the bow and climbed out of my airplane. Helmet in hand, hot and sweaty after a difficult night mission, I was walking down the flight deck toward the ready room. A young sailor stopped me.

"Can I say something, sir?" He asked.

"Sure," I replied.

"You guys have balls!"

11

Flying High

John Magee, Jr. was a young American pilot flying Spitfires with the Royal Canadian Air Force. Sent to England for combat duty in July of 1941, he was killed shortly after composing a poem that eloquently described the exhilaration of high performance flying.

"High Flight"

Oh! I have slipped the surly bonds of earth
And danced the skies on laughter-silvered wings;
Sunward I've climbed, and joined the tumbling mirth
Of sun-split clouds—and done a hundred things
You have not dreamed of—wheeled and soared and swung
High in the sunlit silence. Hov'ring there,
I've chased the shouting wind along, and flung
My eager craft through footless halls of air.
Up, up the long, delirious, burning blue
I've topped the wind-swept heights with easy grace
Where never lark, or even eagle flew—
And, while with silent lifting mind I've trod
The high untrespassed sanctity of space,
Put out my hand and touched the face of God.

John Gillespie Magee, Jr.

I loved Navy flying. The speed, freedom and beauty that I experienced at the controls of a Navy jet fighter are almost indescribable. Some of the training missions that we flew in California were low-level, high speed navigation runs through the Sierra Nevada Mountains. Typically, at speeds approaching 500 miles per hour and an altitude not more than 500 feet above the ground, we would zip through mountain passes and over ridges, navigating toward a simulated enemy target well within the country's interior. The actual high speed pass over the "target" would be at 100 feet above the ground and close to 600 miles per hour. What a kick! The slightest loss of concentration would be disastrous, of course, but when the testosterone is flowing in that "young and stupid" phase of life, invincibility reigns supreme.

Speed is better appreciated when close to stationary objects. For the sheer joy of flying and the intoxication of speed, I would love to skim the valleys of the Sierras, as close to tree-top level as possible. Not everyone was appreciative of these high jinks, however. One summer morning I was listening to a forest ranger lecture about the flora and fauna in Sequoia National Park. My wife and I had spent the night camping under the stars; a couple of black bears had passed within feet of us during the night. Mid-lecture, a Navy jet at tree-top level screamed overhead and disappeared. The jet noise in that thin, mountain air was deafening. The ranger threw down his notes and went on a tirade about the U.S. Navy in general and Navy pilots in particular. I didn't have the guts to tell him that I had pulled the same prank just a few days earlier.

Rudy Kohn was the commanding officer of our squadron, VA-93. He was a well-known, highly decorated naval aviator whose exploits in the Vietnam War were chronicled in several books of the era. Rudy was a leader who inspired trust and led by example. Besides, he was just a hell of a good guy. He even bought my old Chevy Nova with the binding clutch linkage and the sun-faded red paint. His primary criteria in judging the car: it had a useable AM radio.

Prior to my second deployment to Vietnam, our squadron of Corsairs had been operating off the coast of San Francisco, west of the Farralon Islands, practicing carrier landings aboard the USS Midway. We had been at sea for a week and the date for our nine month deployment was fast approaching. One afternoon, our squadron maintenance officer identified two A-7's that required scheduled maintenance at our home base in Lemoore, California. He petitioned the ship for a launch time and the squadron for two volunteers to fly the planes. Rudy and I leaped at the opportunity, knowing that when we got back to the base, our wives would be waiting. At best, we could carve out a couple of extra nights at home.

With little advance notice, the ship's operations officer informed us that the Midway would be available for a thirty minute launch window. I threw some incidentals in a travel bag, climbed into my torso harness, G-suit and survival vest and made my way up the various ladders and passageways to the flight deck. I did a cursory inspection of the exterior of my aircraft, pulled the safety pin on the ejection seat and climbed into the cockpit, my mind probably more on the reunion with my bride than with the task at hand. When I settled into the seat and took my first glance at the instrument panel, I was shocked. One of the major engine instruments, the turbine inlet temperature gauge, was missing. There was a small round hole in the firewall where the gauge should have been!

It was command decision time. If I elected to take a delay to find a replacement gauge and squandered the thirty minute launch time, I would be spending another night aboard ship. If I decided to launch without the gauge, I would be without one of the basic diagnostic tests of engine performance. That engine, after all, was the only thing that kept me from swimming in the cold Pacific Ocean after the ship's catapult fired. I'm ashamed to admit that testosterone trumped judgment. I decided to fly, gauge or no gauge.

Fortunately, the launch was routine. Afterwards, Rudy and I joined up in close formation, struck an easterly course, climbed to a cruising altitude of 25,000 feet and enjoyed the approach of the beautiful California coastline. I'm sure that my thoughts were well ahead of that airplane as I daydreamed about the reunion with my bride.

After landing, I was signing the aircraft logbook in the squadron maintenance office in Lemoore when a Navy chief mechanic, in a fine state of temper, stormed into the office. Ignoring me, he reported to Commander Kohn that Lieutenant Thompson's aircraft didn't even have a turbine gauge installed in it and had flown in that way! Rudy just looked at me and grinned. He had been a newlywed once upon a time...

One flight with Rudy still endures as the most beautiful flight of my life. Four of us had finished a training mission at a bombing range in Nevada and we were on our way back to California, over the Sierras. Our Corsairs were light, most of our fuel had been burned and all of our practice bombs had been dropped. Rudy was in the lead. He signaled us to slip into a trail formation whereby all the airplanes were lined up one behind the other, about fifty feet apart. Rudy smoothly advanced the throttle and began a descent. The three of us followed, maintaining our intervals. He leveled around fifteen thousand feet and accelerated to 400 miles an hour. He was headed directly for a small thunderstorm that was rapidly building over the western edge of the mountains. Just prior to the storm, he pulled his aircraft into a vertical climb and hugged the fringe of that cloud. As he approached the zenith of the storm, he rolled his aircraft inverted and pulled it into a vertical dive on the other side. Each of us, in turn, at an interval of fifty feet, climbed and rolled and dove. It was poetry. John Magee would have approved.

◆   ◆   ◆

If I had been single, I might have pursued a career in the Navy. I loved the flying. The *esprit de corps* and the camaraderie of like-minded aviators were unique. But the cruises, the Navy term for deployments that could vary between nine months and a year, were terrible hardships for young families. While substitute teaching, my wife had observed the discipline problems of the fatherless children of Navy families. We wanted more stability in our family life. And we certainly did not want to produce troubled, undisciplined children for lack of a permanent father figure.

I started writing to airlines in the early 1970's but the prospects of landing a flying job were slim. Most of the major airlines had pilots on furlough status and wouldn't be hiring for the foreseeable future. My five year enlistment would be satisfied in early 1972, just a few short months in the future. I had to come up with a plan.

A college buddy from the University of Illinois called one day and invited me to Chicago for an interview with the chief pilot of North Central Airlines, a regional airline with domiciles in Chicago, Minneapolis and Detroit. Larry Rakunas had finished his university studies at a more leisurely pace than I and had enrolled in an aviation program at Midway Airport in Chicago. After satisfying the minimum requirements for a commercial pilot's license, his brother, who was a captain at North Central, finagled a flying job for him and then petitioned Larry's draft board for a critical skills deferment. His draft board must have been more lenient than mine since Larry now owned an airline seniority number and was flying as a Convair 580 first officer. By virtue of his exemption from the military draft, he was years ahead of me in the airline industry.

I bought a ticket on United Airlines from Fresno to Chicago and planned to talk to the chief pilots of Delta Air Lines and North Central. The interviews never generated any job offers but I did get a chance to spend a night with my folks in Illinois.

It was snowing the day that I planned to return to California so my mother, who was driving me to the airport, allowed an extra hour for the trip. Actually, it took far less time on the uncongested freeways than we had anticipated, so I was early for my flight. With time on my hands, I decided to find the chief pilot of Ozark Airlines, a small Midwestern regional airline to whom I had written.

Jim Frankenburger, a slow-talking, handsome man, read my resume and cover letter. He announced that Ozark hadn't hired any pilots in three years but was about to begin the interview process. Would I care to fly to St. Louis and attend an interview the next morning?

"Yes, sir," I told him.

Captain Frankenburger wrote me a non-revenue pass on an Ozark turboprop 48-passenger airliner that made a stop in Springfield, Illinois, before continuing on to St. Louis. I rented a hotel room near the St. Louis Airport and reported the next morning to the Ozark Airlines company headquarters.

My interview was efficient but brief. Afterwards, Captain Peter Sherwin introduced me to the Vice President of Operations and suggested that I spend the afternoon taking the Stanine Test, a combination aviation knowledge examination and psychological evaluation. In a huge tactical blunder, I begged off and hopped on a TWA flight to San Francisco. I was airborne before I realized that I had made a terrible mistake.

Home again, in California, with about three weeks until my release from active duty, I was still without a plan.

Commander Dave Rogers, an ex-squadron mate from VA-93, called me from Washington. He was temporarily assigned to the Bureau of Naval Personnel. He wanted to know what he could do to convince me to remain in the Navy.

"I love the flying, Dave. It's the cruises that I can't handle."

"If I can find a way around the cruises, would you consider staying?"

"Sure," I told him.

A week later he called again.

"Here's the deal," he said. "You have a B.S. in Physics. What I'm proposing is a tour of duty at the Naval Post Graduate School in Monterrey. You'll earn a Master's in Aeronautical Engineering. From there you'll be assigned to the Navy Test Pilot School in Pax River, Maryland. You'll be involved in the test and development of aircraft and not required to make any more cruises. What do you think?"

I was floored. In the first place, Dave had moved a mountain for me and I was grateful. The Navy had always lived up to its promises and I expected that if I accepted this one, the promise would be kept. Dave was a real gentleman who went on to become commanding officer of the USS Constellation and eventually achieved flag rank. But I turned down his offer because I had this feeling that my destiny lay in a different direction...

At the moment, I had a pregnant wife, no job and no health insurance. Then the next door opened...

The telephone call was from Western Union. A sweet female voice read a telegram from Ozark Airlines: If I could pass a pre-employment physical and could report in two weeks, I was invited to become a member of the next class of Ozark Airlines pilots.

From the end of my active duty in the Navy to the beginning of a career in the airlines, I was out of work less than two weeks.

12

Ozark Airlines

Except for a bout of nervous nausea in Arizona and an ice storm in Oklahoma, the quick trip from California to Missouri was without incident. My pre-employment physical was scheduled for Saturday, January 29th 1972, in St. Louis. Dr. Hattes, Ozark's company physician, provided one of the strangest physical examinations that I have ever experienced. Twice during the course of the exam he asked me what company I was planning to work for.

"Ozark Airlines," I told him, both times.

As I paid his bill, he wished me well.

"I hope that you're very happy at North American Rockwell," he said.

Either he was telling me that I wouldn't be working for Ozark or that his mental state wasn't quite first class. I had initially considered using him as my pregnant wife's obstetrician since we didn't know anyone else in town. But after the physical, I decided against it. It wouldn't surprise me if there had been something approaching 80 proof in one of his desk drawers.

Ozark Airlines, a regional airline headquartered in St. Louis, flew two types of aircraft on a route system that stretched from Denver to New York and from Minneapolis to Miami. The airline had been born in the Midwest in 1950 and still emphasized routes through Missouri, Iowa, Illinois and Minnesota. The McDonald Douglas DC-9 was Ozark's workhorse on the longer routes and the Fairchild FH-227 was the aircraft that puddle-jumped through the smaller towns, feeding connecting traffic to St. Louis or Chicago. During the 1970's Ozark became an all-jet airline and began providing coast-to-coast service to selected cities. Ozark also ran a well-respected charter department that catered to professional sports teams, gambling junkets and sports fans. At its peak, Ozark flew 50 DC-9's of different versions and vintages.

On Monday morning, January 31st 1972, eight pilots, the first group hired by Ozark in three years, began their airline careers in a building just off the end of one of the runways at St. Louis Lambert International Airport. The only ex-military pilot in the group, I was at a disadvantage in ground school because I had very little experience with civilian instrument landing systems. Jim Creighton, a knowledgeable and patient instructor, brought me up to speed with a little private tutoring. Our class was trained to fly the Fairchild Hiller 227B Friendship turboprop airliner, a 48-passenger, under-powered twin engine, high-winged aircraft. All flight training was completed in the actual airplane because simulators weren't yet available.

My landings during training were atrocious. The airplane would hit the ground with such force that it would bounce twenty or thirty feet into the air. Mel Burkhart, my flight instructor, finally figured out the problem. Mel was a Navy reservist in his spare time and recognized that I was using Navy carrier landing techniques to land civilian airplanes. The criterion for a successful landing on an aircraft carrier is to touch down within the 50-foot area of the flight deck that housed the arresting cables. Navy pilots are taught to make every landing on shore and aboard ship the same way: focusing strictly on the optical system that beams the glide slope into space, the pilot flies the aircraft onto the runway and lets the landing gear absorb the shock. The resulting landing is usually very firm, not the kind of touch-down that an airline passenger is expecting. (Occasionally, during my airline career, a knowledgeable passenger, after experiencing a less than perfect landing, would stop by the cockpit on his way off the airplane and ask if I used to be a Navy pilot.) Anyway, Mel taught me the art of flaring, i.e. gradually breaking the descent rate of the aircraft, instead of flying it into the runway. My landings improved.

Except for one young man who failed his post-training check ride in the Fairchild and was fired, the rest of us were either assigned to Ozark's domiciles at Chicago O'Hare or St. Louis. Chicago was the natural choice for me because of my family in northern Illinois and so it happened that I found myself once again in front of Captain Jim Frankenburger, Ozark's chief pilot in Chicago. He told me that I was the first fellow that he had ever sent to an interview who returned with a job. Jim was an easy-going, well-liked administrator and we became friends.

The first year with an airline is probationary. A new first officer is graded by every captain with whom he flies on attitude, flying skills and knowledge of the aircraft. Some crusty old captains who have been flying the same aircraft over the same routes for years had no interest in teaching a new guy the tricks of the trade. To them, I represented a potential threat: someone who was unfamiliar with the Ozark cities and the airline operation. If I were to make a mistake, they might have to answer for it as the pilot in command. They preferred a familiar first officer whom they didn't have to supervise quite so closely. It wasn't unusual for one of these guys to do most of the flying themselves rather than trade flight duties with the first officer.

Other captains were wonderful teachers who would often let me fly every leg of the trip, in good weather and bad. These guys were usually the best pilots in the domicile, comfortable in their abilities and patient teachers.

First year pay was $600 per month for the first six months and $650 for the last six. At the end of the year, a probationary first officer was given a check ride with an instructor pilot. The check ride is like a three dimensional driver's test taken while all the systems of the vehicle are failing. A friend from United Airlines used to euphemistically refer to it as a game called "You Bet Your Career." Of course, the purpose of the check ride is to demonstrate that a pilot is capable of landing and taking off the aircraft in low visibility weather and that he can successfully handle any in-flight emergency, such as engine or electrical failures or fires or loss of pressurization or any combination of the above. It is a high stress examination. But pass the check ride and you become a member of the union and you start earning a reasonable salary. Flunk the check ride and you're looking for a new job.

My first year was relatively uneventful. I quickly learned that no one wanted to hear anything about my military experiences, so I kept my mouth shut. I had been used to flying a single pilot airplane, performing all in-flight procedures myself. The crew concept of sharing flight duties was foreign initially, but it did make sense. The airline divided cockpit chores into those completed by the "flying pilot" or the "non-flying pilot." In other words, one pilot flew the aircraft and commanded the other pilot to raise or lower the landing gear, tune radios or accomplish emergency procedures. The non-flying pilot would talk on the radio and respond to the other pilot's commands. The first officer, when he was the flying pilot, didn't really command anything, of course. He just tactfully suggested and hoped that he didn't break any of the captain's personal rules.

At the end of my first year, I was in the Ozark crew lounge at O'Hare, dressed in civilian clothes, waiting for an instructor. All around me pilots and flight attendants (they called them stewardesses back in the '70's) were in uniform, reporting for and returning from scheduled trips. One of the captains, with whom I'd flown quite a lot during the past year, walked in and asked me why I was dressed in civvies. I told him that I was waiting to go out on my probationary check ride.

"Who's your instructor?" asked Dick Hoover.

"Bob Rowe," I said.

Dick told me to hang loose, that he'd be right back. He disappeared into the chief pilot's office to look for Bob. In a few moments, he was back.

"It's all set," he said. "You have to fly the check ride, but you passed."

To this day I don't know what, if anything, Dick said to Bob but it did break the tension. The check ride was completed satisfactorily and I felt as if a tremendous load had been lifted from my shoulders.

A couple of incidents occurred in the next few years that, had they transpired during my probationary year, they would have resulted in my having had a very brief airline career.

One afternoon, the Vice President of Flight Operations of Ozark Airlines scheduled a meeting with all the pilots of the Chicago domicile. The purpose of the meeting was to give the Chicago pilots a chance to interact with the middle managers of the Flight Operations Department. The Chicago domicile was roughly ten per cent of the entire operation, but we were an island. Except for the benevolent supervision of Jim Frankenburger, we had little contact with management and most of us didn't keep up with internal company politics.

I had felt for some time that the seniority system of the airline was detrimental to the overall operation. Each individual pilot was awarded his choice of aircraft to fly, his seat on that airplane, his monthly schedule, his vacation and his compensation based solely on his system seniority, the date he came to work for the airline. With so much energy focused on maximizing the rights and benefits of the individual, the overall health and vitality of the airline got short shrift. It seemed to me that what the airline needed was more *esprit de corps* and less individualism. Fresh from the Navy, where camaraderie and trust were necessary ingredients for survival, my frame of reference hadn't caught up with the times. I was naive.

When I had a chance to voice some of my concerns at the meeting, I talked of *esprit de corps*, cooperation and unity. My remarks were greeted with polite indifference by the management pilots. The reaction of my fellow pilots was incredulity. Among themselves, the Chicago pilots considered me, at minimum, disloyal and, at maximum, devious and dishonest. By the time the story of my little speech made the rounds of the guys who weren't at the meeting, I was reputed to have accused my fellow pilots of everything from stealing from the company to cheating on their wives. That anyone with so little seniority could have an opinion, much less a criticism, seemed outrageous.

On my subsequent flights, cockpit discussions would sometimes dwell on what was said at that meeting and I would get a chance to explain myself. Joe Floeter, one of the captains with whom I flew during the period shortly after the meeting, counseled me to disregard any heat I took. "Time heals all," he said.

By and large, Joe was right. But there was one Chicago captain who wasn't going to let me off the hook. I began finding notes in my mailbox in the crew lounge. "Zip Your Lip!" was one of the unsolicited messages. Several other crude notes, always in the same handwriting, sent me to the aircraft log books, searching for the author's handwriting. It didn't take long to identify my tormentor: Tom Livingston. For months, the notes continued: childish, insulting and profane.

In October of 1974, I was assigned to fly with Captain Livingston. We were scheduled to stay together as a crew for the entire month.

From our first encounter, it was clear that Tom Livingston had no use for me. The conversation in the cockpit was minimal, just the bare necessities to accomplish the job. To be cooped up in a tiny cockpit with someone who was openly hostile was uncomfortable, but the pay was the same whether Tom liked me or not. I had no illusions that we would ever interact socially. I concentrated on performing my duties professionally and avoided Tom as much as possible.

In mid-month, I was sitting in the cockpit preparing the aircraft for a flight from St. Louis to Decatur, Illinois. I knew that the weather in Decatur was foggy and rainy and that we would need our instrument landing system to get in. I checked out all of the radios and switches on my half of the cockpit (the only half that I was permitted to touch), called STL clearance delivery for our FAA clearance to Decatur and waited for Tom to arrive. He usually plopped into his seat a minute or two before our scheduled departure time, started the engines and taxied out. He didn't believe in check lists or preflight inspections. And he certainly didn't want to spend any more cockpit time with me than he absolutely had to.

True to form, he dropped into his seat a couple of minutes before departure, put on his lap belt, hit me with a disgusted glare, started the engines and taxied out of the chocks. The take-off and climb were normal and we leveled at 7,000 feet. Established in cruise flight, he reached for the clipboard with the flight papers and weather reports. Out of the corner of my eye I could see that he was just now discovering that Decatur was going to be a problem. He looked up from the weather report and noticed that there was a red warning flag in one of the instruments on his flight panel. Without that particular instrument, it wouldn't be possible to land in the fog. Tom tapped on the gauge, checked various circuit breakers and finally discovered that his main navigation radio was simply turned off. He flipped it on and the red warning flag disappeared.

There was silence for a long moment. Then he turned to me.

"Did you know that that radio was turned off?" He asked.

"Yes sir."

Another even longer moment of silence passed. I knew that he was deep in thought but I had no idea where he was going.

Said Tom, "I think it's time we buried the hatchet."

From that moment, I became his buddy. Tom was a very intelligent man but he habitually made stupid decisions in his private life. He was a chronic trouble-maker on the job, just skirting discipline or termination by virtue of his quick wit and his innate audacity. He was just a little too slippery to be caught.

After half a month of silence during our trips together, suddenly I couldn't get Tom to shut up. He told me more than I wanted to know about his personal life, gave me advice on many subjects and complained at length about Ozark Airlines.

After Decatur, our trip continued to Champaign, Illinois, then up to Chicago, back to Champaign and then finally finished in Chicago. During the conversation that afternoon, I mentioned that my parents were in Champaign visiting my brother, who was a student at the University of Illinois. They were scheduled to be on the flight from Champaign to Chicago just prior to ours.

Tom became animated. He told me to call my folks and tell them to wait for our flight to Chicago. I did. I called my dad and he readily agreed. They were traveling on my parental non-revenue passes issued by Ozark, so they might just as well ride on their son's flight.

Later, at the Champaign airport, I introduced Captain Livingston to my parents. They had no idea that for the last six months, he had been my private scourge. We settled my folks into their seats on the airplane and then Tom asked my dad if he wanted to look at the cockpit. He brought him forward, strapped him into the jump seat between our seats and winked at me. My buddy, Tom, troublemaker *extraordinaire*, was about to entertain an unauthorized guest in the cockpit.

Dad must have thought that riding in the cockpit was a normal courtesy that the crew could extend to almost anyone but, in truth, it was highly forbidden to have anyone in the cockpit during flight who did not have appropriate credentials. But there he sat. We started the engines, taxied to the runway and took off for Chicago. During climb and cruise, we explained the various navigation and aircraft systems and answered Dad's questions. On the approach to O'Hare International Airport, sitting above and behind us, he had a wonderful view of the multi-runway operation of the world's busiest airport. About a mile off of our left side, a jetliner was landing on a runway parallel to our own. Two other runways were being used for take-offs, intersecting our landing runway, but timed to avoid conflict. As usual, it was aerial ballet performed by the best air traffic controllers in the business. And my father had a front row seat for the performance, thanks to an ex-enemy named Tom Livingston.

Tom's airline career eventually came to an ignominious end. He was overnighting in Kansas City one night and decided to rent a car. Pulled over for driving under the influence of alcohol, he gave the arresting trooper some grief and landed in jail. He used his one phone call to tell Ozark that he was sick for his scheduled departure in the morning. When Mothers Against Drunk Drivers, MADD, discovered that an airline pilot was a drunk driver and complained to Ozark about it, management finally had the ammunition it needed to terminate Tom. His years of bad behavior and flaunting the system finally cost him his job, and eventually, his life.

◆   ◆   ◆

Petulant and moody, Paul Walsh (not his real name) was the indulged son of a wealthy dentist. Paul started with Ozark at an opportune time. Expanding rapidly, Ozark hired many classes of pilots after him and Paul soon found himself promoted to captain, in accordance with the seniority system.

One of Paul's favorite sports was walking into a crowded crew lounge in Chicago or St. Louis, spreading some sort of volatile, ridiculous un-truth, getting everyone involved in discussing and arguing about it, and then leaving. He was a talented trouble maker who could exude charm or venom depending on the opportunity.

I had flown with Paul enough to know that he had certain idiosyncrasies and that he could be very volatile if he felt threatened. He was a chronic complainer and entertained exactly one point of view: his own. Once upon a time, I had taken my wife with me on a Kansas City layover. On the early morning cab ride to the airport she was sitting between Paul and me, bubbling about how much fun the trip had been. I stole a glance at Paul and I knew from his squirming that he was exasperated. I had neglected to brief my wife that one doesn't talk to Paul in the morning until either he has had more than one cup of coffee or it's after eight o'clock.

Catherine was the nice lady who worked the front desk at the Prom Sheraton Hotel in downtown Kansas City. The Ozark crews were regulars there and she came to know many of us by name and face. I could usually rely on her to find me a room with a Thermasol steam bath, if one were available. The hotel must have made a good buy on some wine because Catherine would give each crew member a bottle when he or she checked in. We weren't expected to drink the stuff in the hotel, but I did accumulate an impressive collection in a cabinet at home, each bottle representing a night's stay at the Prom Sheraton. One afternoon, Paul and crew checked in with Catherine and headed toward the elevators to find their rooms. Noticing that Paul had left his bottle of wine sitting on the counter, Catherine called across the lobby.

"Captain Walsh! You forgot your bottle of wine, sir."

Paul was embarrassed. An airline captain in full uniform publicly reminded to take his bottle of wine with him to his room! He reacted badly, but in true form. Rather than handling his discomfort in a quiet, adult manner, he made enough of a fuss with Catherine and her boss that none of us ever received any future gratuities from the Prom Sheraton.

Overall, the maintenance reliability of the airlines is head and shoulders above the military's. Of course the missions of naval aviation and Ozark Airlines are vastly different. It was not unusual to fly for months without having anything seriously wrong with the mechanical condition of an airliner. There were other times, however, when it seemed that all of the aircraft were infected with some strange virus. They all seemed to get sick at once.

Murphy's Law dictates that if anything CAN go wrong, it WILL go wrong. That certainly could have been the motto of the month for June of 1976. Paul Walsh and I were flying as a crew and it seemed that whichever airplane we flew, some vital system would break down and our trip would cancel. Radios failed or landing gear wouldn't indicate properly or engines would signal that they were on fire and bells would ring. It seemed that we were running more emergency check lists than normal check lists. Not only was it frustrating that we couldn't seem to get where we were supposed to go, but our paychecks were taking a hit every time we cancelled a flight for mechanical reasons.

On June 23rd we landed in Ottumwa, Iowa, our last stop before Kansas City and the end of our day. On touchdown, the fire warning system on the left engine illuminated and the fire bell rang. Since we were already on the ground, Paul shut off the fuel to that engine and a moment later, the fire indications stopped. We taxied to the gate, disgusted that another mechanical problem was about to ruin our schedule.

Paul shut down the remaining engine, popped out of his seat and walked back through the passenger compartment. I finished my paperwork and started after him. I assumed that he would either tell one of the ticket agents about our problem or go into the terminal to call maintenance or dispatch. He did neither. He slowly walked around the left engine and glared at it as if he could determine from the outside of the cowling whether all was well internally. After some moments of walking and glaring, he reboarded the aircraft and returned to the cockpit. I didn't like the looks of this.

The fire warning system of a jet engine is basically a set of cables that run around the exterior of the engine and underneath the cowl. The cables are calibrated to sense temperature above a certain value and to complete a circuit to the cockpit, indicating that something on that engine is too hot, possibly on fire. While not totally reliable, it's the only system that can warn the pilots of a catastrophic fire before structural damage to the fuel-filled wing is affected. A fuel line to the engine could have broken, dumping raw kerosene on the hot sections of the engine or an engine duct could have vibrated loose, spewing hot turbine air over the sensor cables. Or the cables themselves could be defective. But the only way to know for sure is to have a qualified mechanic take a look.

I stepped into the lavatory to gather my thoughts. Why hadn't Paul told the agent of our situation? Something like this usually results in a substantial delay and sometimes the cancellation of the flight. I had an inkling of what was coming.

I walked up to the cockpit and stood between the seats.

"So what do you think, Paul?" I asked.

"I think we'll start the engine and see if the fire warning comes on," he said.

"What are you going to do if the warning *doesn't* come on?"

"I think we'll just continue on to Kansas City," he said.

"I don't think that's a good idea, Paul."

"Well," he said, "I don't care what you think!"

"Then you'll have to go to Kansas City by yourself," I replied.

I had drawn the line in the sand and Paul knew it. I had forced his hand and now he had to do something about it. He exploded out of his seat and stormed into the terminal to make phone calls. For all I knew, he was arranging for my death by firing squad for challenging the authority of an airline captain. I was out of the loop for the moment. All I could do was wait to see what happened next.

As I found out later, Paul had had a lengthy conversation with Jim Frankenburger, probably about me, and then called the Ozark dispatcher working our flight to arrange for a maintenance evaluation of our fire warning system. A mechanic flew in from another Ozark station, tore the engine apart and replaced the defective fire warning system. Our Kansas City trip was cancelled and Paul and I ferried the empty airplane to St. Louis for further repairs.

Communication in the cockpit after our incident was minimal and icy. Captain Paul Walsh did not like me. We rode an Ozark DC-9 from St. Louis to Chicago and then went home. Our two day trip had been cut in half again.

I flew another trip with Paul on the 28th and 29th. He was his hateful self and refused to talk to me. By the time the trip was over on the second day, I was feeling pretty low. I happened to meet another one of our captains, a big ex-cop, on the way to my car and he made a point of telling me that had I done to him what I had done to Paul, he would have thrown me off the flight and had me replaced. OK, now I was really low. Apparently everyone in the domicile knew about my rebellion and disapproved.

I had just walked into my kitchen at home when the phone rang. It was Buzz Wendzel, the head of our Chicago pilots union. He told me that he had heard about my situation with Paul.

"How did you hear, Buzz?" I had told no one about the incident, preferring to believe that Paul had just suffered from a momentary loss of judgment.

"Paul has been telling everyone how you tried to countermand his authority," said Buzz. "I just wanted to tell you that you were right and he was wrong. If there's any company trouble over this incident, the union is going to back you. I just wanted you to know."

I thanked him for the call and felt like the weight of the world was off my shoulders. Suddenly, I was angry. For two weeks I had put up with Paul's guff and the humiliation he had stirred up among our fellow pilots, and all for a mistake in judgment that was his own. I picked up the phone and dialed Paul's number.

His wife answered. I told her who I was and that I wanted to talk to that "no-good husband of hers."

When Paul came on the line, I dredged up every insult to his parentage and courage that I could recall and told him that if there was any more trouble over our Ottumwa incident, "it was going to be his tit in the wringer, not mine." And then I hung up...I was scheduled to fly with him the next morning.

I was in the crew lounge when he walked in. I didn't know what to expect. He came in, threw his arm around my shoulder and said, "Let me buy you a cup of coffee." He knew he'd been had. He turned on the charm and reemerged as my friend, as if there had never been a conflict between us.

I flew again with Paul many times after that and we got along fine. But I knew what he was and he knew better than to test me. It wasn't a bad relationship.

13

Captain

Ed Thompson was the Federal Aviation Association air carrier inspector assigned to Ozark Airlines. He accompanied the Ozark pilots on their normal passenger flights, supervised their training, and spot checked maintenance compliance with FAA standards. He was a qualified airman who was type-rated (captain qualified) on both the Fairchild turboprop and the McDonald Douglas DC-9. Ed had completed the Ozark ground school courses on company flight policies and procedures and was sufficiently knowledgeable to judge a pilot's performance from an FAA or an Ozark perspective.

Typically, Ed would arrive unannounced, standing inconspicuously in the cockpit doorway during the passenger boarding process. He would greet both pilots and then settle into the jump seat between us. He'd sit quietly, observing all aspects of a normal flight from the prestart engine check list to the take-off, cruise, landing and eventual arrival at the destination gate. Officially, he was the FAA's enforcer, capable of levying fines or revoking airman certificates if he witnessed any violation of FAA rules or procedures.

Ed and I shared the same last name but we weren't related. I would pass him off as my "Uncle Ed" to a few of the captains with whom I flew and he would play along. He was an easy-going veteran of the Korean Conflict, a decorated infantry officer who discovered aviation after his release from the Army.

I met Ed for the first time on the evening of December 30th, 1974. The occasion was my annual first officer check ride. Captains are required to demonstrate their flight proficiency every six months and first officers annually. Since Ozark didn't own a simulator for the Fairchild, the 48-passenger turboprop aircraft that served Ozark's smaller cities, all of the check rides were flown in the actual aircraft and were scheduled during the middle of the night, after the airplanes were no longer needed for passenger service. The one advantage of late night training was that seldom did an FAA inspector show up to observe. As far as the pilots were concerned, the check rides were sufficiently tense without having the FAA looking over our shoulders. And then Ed became the air carrier inspector. He was conscientious, motivated and wanted to observe every aspect of the Ozark operation. That particular night, he looked like he hadn't shaved in a couple of days, but there he was, sitting on the jump seat watching as my instructor failed engines and quizzed me on emergency actions or instrument flight procedures in the night skies above St. Louis.

In May of 1977, Ozark published a list of first officers who were to be promoted to Captain. My name was on the list. I was given a class date to begin the training process that, if successful, would entitle me to sew a fourth stripe on my uniform coat, move from the first officer position in the cockpit to the coveted left seat and increase my pay by at least thirty per cent.

At its peak, the seniority list of Ozark Airlines contained the names of 550 pilots. There were the usual three per cent of trouble makers and malcontents, but the rest of us had established reputations as capable aviators and responsible employees. The incompetent first officers had usually been eliminated by the end of their probationary year. If a pilot's professional reputation was respectable, upgrading from first officer to captain was a relatively stress-free event.

The FAA requires that each captain be type-rated on the particular airplane that he will command. That means, for example, that a Fairchild 227 captain must demonstrate to the FAA by means of an oral examination that he knows and understands each subsystem of the aircraft, e.g. pneumatics, electrical, fire protection, engines, navigation, ice and rain protection, fuel, flight controls, communications, air conditioning, flight instruments, etc. Then the prospective captain is required to demonstrate in the aircraft that he can handle any sort of mechanical failure, emergency situation or combination thereof.

For the flight training, the instructor pilot would sit in the first officer's seat, the student captain would be in the left seat and the FAA examiner would sit between us, observing and injecting comments or questions. If both the oral examination and the flight check ride are satisfactory, the FAA awards the student captain an airline transport rating, a license to act as captain of that particular type of aircraft in flight. In many ways, the traditions and prerequisites of sea captains flavor the grooming of an airline captain.

After satisfying the requirements of the FAA, the student captain is still some distance from the responsibility, glory and pay of the pilot in command position. He must now prove to his airline that he can safely perform the duties of a captain in normal passenger service, observing the myriad of company rules and restrictions. A check airman will ride with the new captain for the first twenty-five flight hours of normal airline operations, serving as his first officer, but in fact training him and observing his command of the operation. Judgment, knowledge, flight technique and crew coordination are all graded aspects of the line check. It is not terribly unusual for a student captain to satisfy the FAA requirements for the rating but fail miserably on the practical aspects of the job. One Ozark student captain was required to endure over 160 hours of line checking and never did satisfy the company that his judgment was adequate. He continued his career as a first officer.

My oral exam with Ed Thompson was straightforward and efficient. Ed had a few points that he liked to stress, but I think he enjoyed teaching more than quizzing.

Captain Joe Barker was the check pilot assigned to bring me up to proficiency in the left seat and then conduct the type rating check ride with Ed observing. Joe was an easy-going guy in his late thirties with triplets at home. He used to joke that once the flight attendants found out that he had triplets, they would avoid him as aggressively as if he were infected with VD. Joe and I flew two practice sessions with me sitting in the left seat. Since I had flown the airplane for almost seven years from the right seat, it was just a matter of teaching my right hand to do what my left hand used to. Ed came along on the third flight, observed that all of the maneuvers and practice emergencies were successfully completed and extended the official benediction of the FAA.

We had been using the airport at Cape Girardeau, Missouri, as our practice field for the instrument approaches and landings and Joe decided to refuel our aircraft before returning to St. Louis. Since my FAA training was now officially complete, he asked Ed if he'd like to fly the Fairchild on the way home. Ed jumped at the chance. I climbed out of the captain's seat, went back into the cabin and became a passenger. I was feeling almost as good as I did that summer's day back in 1966 when I earned my private pilot's certificate.

Later, I was standing in the cockpit as Ed taxied the airplane to the parking spot in St. Louis, shut down the engines and set the brakes.

"I can do this job," he said. Secretly, I think that's exactly what Ed would have liked.

My line check instructor was a pilot named Al Wilson (not his real name). Al was an ex-baseball player who was quite a jock in his youth but his athletic eating habits no longer fit his sedentary life style. Over the course of his airline career his weight and girth continued to balloon until it became a mystery as to how he managed to fit his 350 pound bulk into an airline seat. We used to joke that as long as we used his FAA doctor for our flight physicals, we'd never run the risk of being medically grounded.

I flew with Al for about twenty-five flight hours carrying passengers around the countryside. He crammed himself into the copilot's seat and performed the first officer's duties. I was flying from the captain's seat, supposedly making the decisions and being evaluated. Actually, Al was very much in charge of the operation and I just deferred to whatever he suggested. There was no danger of making a bad decision…I never made any decisions. At the end of our last flight together, he told me that I had done a fine job and wished me well. I was now officially a fully-qualified Ozark Airline captain, albeit on a very primitive airplane.

◆   ◆   ◆

Airlines maintain a reserve pool of qualified pilots and flight attendants to cover any last minute flight requirements or to replace any crew members who become ill or unavailable because of weather or aircraft mechanical problems. In August of 1979, I became a reserve captain whose primary mission was to be available to fly on short notice. Some pilots prefer reserve duty because it can mean less time flying and more time at home but the disadvantage, of course, is that you can never commit to a personal obligation. The phone could ring at any moment with a flight assignment.

That first month I flew about fifty-five hours, about three quarters of a normal month. The flight hour clock, our unit for pay purposes, began ticking when the aircraft door closed and the airplane started moving under its own power. Time spent waiting around airports in crew lounges or passenger boarding areas counted not at all. It was not unusual in the 1970's to spend an entire day earning an hour and a half's flight pay.

On September 2nd, Mark Ameel was my copilot. We were scheduled to operate flight 819 from Chicago O'Hare to Peoria, Illinois, and then continue to St. Louis. The fog was thick over northern Illinois that morning and visibility was reduced to about an eighth of a mile, far too restrictive for landings. An eighth of a mile is adequate for a take-off, provided that there is an airport within an hour's flight distance that is available in the event of an emergency. Peoria was reporting good visibility so Mark and I loaded our assigned passengers, started the engines and began the slow and anxious process of navigating O'Hare's maze of taxiways to the take-off runway. Taxiing around a congested airport in the fog is a potentially dangerous endeavor. If a taxiing aircraft were to stray onto a patch of concrete that someone else is using for a take-off run, the resulting collision would be cataclysmic. The worst aviation disaster of all time occurred in the Canary Islands when two fully loaded Boeing 747's collided on a foggy runway, largely due to a verbal misunderstanding between pilots and air traffic controllers.

I drove the airplane and Mark double checked our position from taxiway signs and the airport map that he held in his hand. From the paucity of radio traffic, we knew that we were the only ones moving on the airfield. When we arrived at the end of Runway 32 Left, the tower controller cleared us for take-off. We rolled onto the runway, lined up on the high intensity center line lights that disappeared into the fog, brought the engines up to take-off power and accelerated. We could only see one or two lights ahead of us but it was enough to allow us to stay centered on the runway as our speed increased. Mark called "Vee 1," our no-go decision speed, and I rotated the Fairchild into the clouds. He retracted our landing gear and we were on our way. We could see absolutely nothing out of the cockpit windows, but our flight instruments were functioning normally, and in just a few moments, we expected to pop out of the fog and into the early morning sunshine.

About fifteen hundred feet above O'Hare and still in the clouds, the right engine suddenly failed. The nose of the aircraft immediately yawed to the right, toward the dead engine and our airspeed started decreasing. I kicked in full left rudder to counteract the yaw and lowered the nose to maintain our altitude and preserve our airspeed. Mark could see the propeller on the right engine from his window and he told me that it had "auto-feathered." In other words, the propeller had rotated its pitch to an angle that caused the least amount of drag in flight.

Speculating that there had been a failure of the "auto-feather safety mechanism," I restarted the engine. The nose yawed back to the left as the engine began producing thrust and I compensated by removing some of the left rudder control that I had been holding. I remember thinking at the time that the people in the cabin must be wondering why on earth their airplane is making these strange gyrations so early in the morning. And then the engine quit again.

By now Mark and I had reconciled to the fact that we were flying an airplane with only one operational engine. We completed the appropriate emergency procedures and check lists and discussed our options. Mark reported to the air traffic controller that we had suffered an engine failure and declared emergency status. There was no possible way that we could return for a landing at O'Hare, Chicago Midway Airport or anywhere else in the northern Illinois area because of the widespread fog. We set a course for Peoria, cruising at 2,500 feet and 165 miles per hour, the best performance we could nurse out of the remaining engine.

When the workload had eased a bit and I felt that we had addressed all of our immediate concerns, I picked up the PA handset and took a moment to compose my thoughts. I firmly believed in being truthful with the passengers but I didn't want to overly alarm them. I took a deep breath and began talking.

I explained that one of our engines had failed but that the airplane was fully capable of flying to a safe destination with the remaining power. I mentioned something to the effect that Lindberg had flown to Paris on one engine and, by God, we could certainly fly to Peoria. I offered everyone a free cocktail and hung up the PA.

Mark and I settled in for the long, slow cruise to Peoria. Because we had so much available time, we completed all of the emergency check lists a couple more times. We discussed the various procedures that we'd be using to make the single engine landing and tried to preplan all contingencies, much the same way that we practiced during our check rides.

About twenty miles north of Peoria the fog dissipated and we could see the ground. It had taken us fifty-five minutes to fly the hundred and fifty miles from Chicago, an Ozark single-engine endurance record that still stands. The landing was uneventful but we were greeted by the airport emergency fire equipment, some Air National Guard vehicles and local TV cameras. With a little more time in the air I'm sure that we could have had reception committees from the Sierra Club and the Young Republicans. We taxied to the terminal and turned our frazzled passengers, all nineteen of them, over to the press. I went inside to take a call from Ozark's Director of Flight Operations, Rich Roberts.

In flight, the pilot in command can choose any course of action that he feels is prudent for the safety of his passengers, crew and airplane. But once on the ground, he must be prepared for the second guessing and the criticism that may require him to defend his actions.

Rich wanted to know the facts. I related the entire incident to him. I was concerned that, as a brand new captain, I had overlooked something important during the course of the emergency or that I had broken some obscure FAA regulation. But Rich was supportive and promised to send some mechanics to evaluate the aircraft. He asked Mark and me to stay with the airplane and work with the troubleshooter when he arrived.

Later that afternoon, Mark and I were in the cockpit again. A mechanic from Chicago sat between us on the jump seat as we went through our normal "Before Engine Start Checklist." We started both the right and the left engines and all cockpit indications were normal. Mechanics love to embarrass pilots by pointing out obvious solutions ("Did you happen to notice that this little itty-bitty circuit breaker was out, Captain?") I was beginning to wonder if our engine problem was going to be one of those "unable to duplicate on the ground" situations where the mechanics chalked up the problem to the pilot's imagination or stupidity.

Peoria ground control allowed us to taxi to a remote area of the airport and we put the right engine through its paces. We ran it at take-off power, idle power and every setting in between. We advanced the throttle rapidly and slowly and did everything imaginable to test it. It functioned normally in every respect. Finally, the mechanic had seen enough. "Let's go back," he said.

I taxied back to our parking spot feeling as if my credibility was mortally wounded. As I rolled to a stop and set the brakes, the right engine shut down all...by...itself. Vindicated, Mark and I left the aircraft with the mechanic and went to a hotel. We had had enough fun for one day.

The next morning we were back at the airport. The plan was to ferry our repaired aircraft to St. Louis, where it could be incorporated into the daily schedule. Maintenance had replaced a faulty fuel control unit on the right engine and it was supposed to be ready on our arrival.

We walked into the Ozark operations area in the Peoria airport and were immediately informed that the right engine had "seized" and that the aircraft was going nowhere. It took some time to get the full story but it turned out that the mechanics had changed the fuel control unit on the engine but had neglected to check the throttle position when they test started the engine. The throttle had been fully open, instead of in the idle position. When fuel and ignition were applied to the engine, it created a fire within the combustion chambers that cooked the engine bearings. Flames would have shot out of the tailpipe, providing quite a light show for any nearby observers.

◆   ◆   ◆

The relationship between pilots and mechanics is generally cordial, but often tense. When a pilot criticizes a faulty aircraft system, a mechanic can choose to believe that his work is being questioned or that a pilot has operated the airplane improperly. But there is another dynamic at work between pilots and mechanics in the airline industry: jealousy.

Navy jet mechanics had their share of frustrations. Parts were always scarce, salt water corrosion was a perpetual nuisance and the nature of the mission was just plain destructive to airplanes. But they were always proud to do what they could to keep the airplanes flying and they never envied the pilots who took those planes into battle. Even though the officer pilots made more money than the enlisted mechanics, I never detected any jealousy of our job description. And I never heard of any jet mechanics becoming prisoners of war at the Hanoi Hilton.

Airline mechanics, on the other hand, considered their contribution to the airline's operation to be as valuable as the pilots', just not nearly so well compensated. Mechanics viewed us as spoiled Prima Donnas who complained about everything while, in fact, enjoying the best of everything. After all, we were the guys in the fancy uniforms who caught the admiring glances from the passengers, spent our days and nights with the beautiful flight attendants and ate crew meals while the autopilot flew the airplane. I never really cared what the mechanics thought of me as long as they performed the required maintenance and told me the truth. It was an attitude acquired through experience.

One morning at O'Hare, we were performing our cockpit preflight checks when the first officer discovered that the aircraft battery was defective. He called it to my attention and I watched while he went through the procedure of isolating the battery, putting an electrical load on it and reading the resulting voltage. I agreed with his conclusion and radioed operations, requesting a mechanic be dispatched to the cockpit. When he arrived, the first officer repeated the battery test procedure for his benefit and the mechanic walked off, presumably to find and install a new battery.

Nothing happened for twenty minutes but the clock was ticking down to departure time. I called operations on the radio and asked if they were making any progress getting a new battery to us. I expected to hear that someone was on his way from the hangar, on the other side of the airport, with a new battery and that it would be installed shortly. Instead, the ops man radioed that a mechanic was on his way to talk to me.

I must have looked like a school boy to the sixtyish, grizzled old mechanic who stepped onto the Fairchild flight deck that morning.

"What seems to be the problem, Captain?" He asked.

"I explained it to the other guy," I said. "Our battery is shot. I thought that a new one was on the way."

And then I got suspicious.

"Just what is your function here?"

"Well," he said, "We don't have any spare batteries and I'm here to convince you that this one is OK."

He went on to explain, perfectly logically, that it's normal for a battery to indicate a low voltage early in the morning and that after an hour of charging in a normal operation, it would be just fine. I had flown this airplane for over eight years and had never seen such a depleted battery, but somehow I fell for his line of bullshit and agreed to fly the airplane as it was. He promised me that by the time we completed our first leg of the day, the battery voltage would test normal.

At the end of that first leg, the battery was still discharged. We checked it again on our second stop and again in St. Louis. I wrote it up in the aircraft logbook and then observed as a St. Louis mechanic removed the battery from the airplane and examined the individual cells. Two thirds of the cells were dry and totally incapable of accepting a charge. If we had needed that battery for emergency power in flight, it would have been absolutely useless.

A good friend and fellow captain, Jon Bollman, once explained his philosophy of the job. He told me that he regarded himself as the final protector of the safety of his passengers. It was Jon's job, and every captain's, to keep aircraft mechanical problems, dangerous weather conditions or even company pressure to complete the mission from threatening the safety of his cargo and crew. I had failed this time around, but I learned a lesson...Never again would I trust anyone else's judgment at the expense of my own.

In September of 1980, Ozark became an all-jet airline and sold the Fairchild turboprops to a European company. I didn't have the seniority to become a DC-9 captain so I was retrained as a DC-9 first officer, flying to some of the more distant Ozark cities like San Diego, Denver, Miami, New York, Washington, Atlanta and New Orleans. The DC-9 was a wonderful airplane with performance that was similar to the A-7's. It would cruise at 35,000 feet at airspeed of almost 8 miles per minute, depending on the jet stream winds. The food service was certainly better than the Fairchild box lunches and there were three flight attendants to fuss over us in the cockpit. Life was good.

I missed the status of being the pilot in command and the freedom to solve problems in my own way, but DC-9 copilot pay was roughly equivalent to Fairchild captain pay and I was flying with some of the most knowledgeable airmen of the airline, gaining experience that would one day serve me well.

Four years later, in the fall of 1984, Butch Gorman and I were in DC-9 captain school. Ground school was taught by Mark Franklin, an ex-mechanic with a wry sense of humor and a chip on his shoulder concerning overpaid airline pilots. Butch didn't help matters when he announced one day in the classroom that he had been working for Ozark for twelve years and hadn't saved a penny. Not to worry, though. He'd just arranged to give tennis lessons to a banker friend in exchange for financial advice. He was planning a life of austerity, living on next to nothing, and was going to save a hundred thousand dollars over a three year period. He would drive his clutch-less old Mazda forever and never spend the money for a new car. I saw him a month later in his brand new Porsche.

Butch was a certifiable character, the most entertaining man I've ever known. But he did cut quite a swath on the airline. In fact, he was notorious among the flight attendants of many airlines for his extra-curricular womanizing. An ex-marine helicopter gunner in Vietnam and a natural athlete, Butch's non-stop chatter and stream of lusty jokes would either charm or disgust his audience. There was no middle ground with Butch Gorman: you either loved him or you hated him.

Much of the flight training for the DC-9 type rating was given in a flight simulator. Obviously, there was a tremendous cost saving over using an airplane but it was also much safer. Many of the maneuvers that we practiced in that simulator would have been quite dangerous in a real airplane in the vicinity of other air traffic. Low ceilings and visibility could easily be programmed into the simulator's visual presentation with realistic results. When flight simulators first started appearing in the sixties and seventies, pilots used to comment that they flew very much like an airplane. Several generations of simulators later, it wasn't unusual to make a low visibility approach and landing in a real airplane and comment afterward that it looked and felt just like the simulator.

My FAA oral examination and type rating check ride went smoothly and a couple of the more volatile check airmen supervised my company line check. October of 1984 was my first month as an Ozark DC-9 captain. It was wonderful to be in command again. The first officers I flew with during that month are still good friends: Bob Ritchie, Rick Cutler, Paul Pickering, Ralph Erickson, Lou Lippi, Gary Custard and Hugh Reynolds. Good men, all.

In November and December I returned to first officer status because the company had an excess of DC-9 captains. In late December, Ozark again ran out of qualified captains and I was moved up to fly as a reserve captain. My first trip was a four day charter flying football fans to various bowl games in different parts of the country.

On the 17th of January, First Officer Mike Kleckner, three flight attendants and I left St. Louis on a two day trip with stops in Dallas and Tampa and an overnight stay in Sarasota. We arrived in Sarasota too late in the evening to enjoy the Florida sun but since we weren't scheduled to leave until early afternoon, we had time for a leisurely breakfast the next morning and a few hours around the hotel swimming pool. It was a nice break from winter in the Midwest.

The Sarasota airport didn't have jetways built into the terminal in 1985. The airliners parked on concrete slabs a short distance from the terminal building. The passengers would descend the aircraft steps, walk across the ramp in a supervised parade and then climb a stairway into the terminal. With the exception of a station manager, Ozark didn't have ground personnel on the field. All ticketing services, cargo loading and paperwork were provided by United Airlines. Any required maintenance could be contracted from local sources but there were absolutely no DC-9 aircraft parts at the airport. Our flight documents were transmitted over United's teletype printers and then collated into a neat package by their operations personnel. One of the United lady load planners used to apply a fresh coat of lipstick and then plant a big red kiss on the top sheet of the Ozark paperwork. It was a Sarasota trademark.

Shortly after noon, Mike and I were at the airport. I reviewed and signed the appropriate flight releases and weather briefing sheets and went outside to stand in the warm sunshine with Mike while we waited for our airplane to arrive from St. Louis. We saw the green and white Ozark DC-9 land to the northwest, decelerate on the runway and taxi towards us. When it rolled to a stop on the ramp, the ground crew straddled the nose tire with chocks. The flight crew shut down the engines, reducing the noise pollution to a more tolerable level. Almost immediately, the forward aircraft door opened and the moveable stairs lurched out of the side of the aircraft, reaching for the concrete. The first officer, Bill Strand, came running down the steps, threw a quick "Hi, Rog" at me and walked rapidly around the nose of the aircraft toward the right wing, eventually completing a clockwise circuit of the entire airplane. From my vantage point at the bottom of the steps I could see a screaming male passenger in the galley, obviously very upset about something. As Bill was about to reboard the aircraft I grabbed him by the arm.

"What in the hell is going on?" I asked him.

"I don't know what happened," he said, "but we hit really hard. The captain is in the process of writing up the aircraft for a hard landing."

Every aircraft has structural design limits based on weight, wing loading, moment arms and other technical criteria. When a pilot suspects that an airplane may have been over-stressed, he is obligated to have maintenance investigate. The nature of aviation accidents is replete with examples of specific aircraft components that didn't fail when first abused, but sometime later to a new crew who had no idea that a problem existed.

The inbound captain, Jim Robertson, was a very senior pilot, just a few years from retirement. He pushed his way through the melee that was still going on in the forward galley, descended the aircraft steps and walked over to me. The aircraft logbook was tucked under his arm.

"The bottom just dropped out from under us," he said. "I've never had a hard landing before, but I'm afraid this one was. Sorry."

He handed me the log and I read his curt entry: "Hard Landing in Sarasota."

Log entries are notoriously brief, just the facts. His entry was on the pilot's side of the page. Across from what he had written was a blank area reserved for maintenance to detail whatever action they would take to correct the problem. It was blank at the moment and until the aircraft was inspected for damage and a notation to that effect put into the logbook, we were stuck in Sarasota. Captain Robertson walked into the United operations area to call St. Louis. I turned my attention back to the fight in the galley.

An attorney was traveling with his pregnant secretary and was loudly berating the airline and the crew for the potential damage to the unborn child. When he discovered that he was going to have to file and sign a claim for damages and run the risk that his wife discover who the father of the child was, he decided to end the discussion and exit with the other passengers.

On the premise that we might actually fly this airplane, Mike had been walking around the outside of it, inspecting it for any obvious problems. He called me over to the left wheel assembly and pointed to the outboard tire. Something had cut the tire and produced four finger-sized strips of rubber that protruded from the thick rubber tread. It certainly didn't look normal or healthy. If you pulled on the individual fingers you could see that the cut was deep into the retread.

By now the inbound captain was back. He handed me the logbook and waited while I read. On the maintenance side of the page, he had written: "Hard Landing Written in Error. Landing was within Limits." And he had signed his name.

I looked at him for an explanation.

"I talked to Al and he asked me what the sink rate was at touchdown. I told him that I wasn't looking at the vertical speed gauge when we landed. I was looking out the window."

"Well, what was the vertical speed the last time you checked it?" Al had asked.

Al Wilson, my old line check captain from the Fairchild days, was now the assistant chief pilot.

"Oh, probably around 600 feet per minute."

"That's within limits. There was no hard landing," Al proclaimed. "Just write in the logbook that the hard landing entry was a mistake."

With the stroke of Jim's pen, I inherited an airplane that he had bashed into the runway with sufficient force to make passengers and crew question its structural integrity. Unbelievable!

I showed Jim Robertson the damaged tire. He wasn't impressed.

"I never saw that before. That's something you'll have to deal with."

Now it was my turn to talk to Al.

I went inside and dialed the number. I explained the condition of the tire and laid out my concerns.

A tire on an airliner is most probably a retread. Financially, it makes much more sense to recap a useable tire carcass than to insist on brand new merchandise every time a tire has to be replaced for tread wear. There are strict criteria for judging the airworthiness of tire tread but when the cap is damaged, you're left guessing whether it will maintain its integrity on a high speed take-off.

The runway at Sarasota was terribly short by airline standards. In order to lift a full load of passengers and fuel we would have to make a high speed, low flap setting take-off. The tires would be subjected to 200 mile per hour speeds just before lift off and the heat buildup on the tire carcass would be considerable. If a retread cap were to let go, it could very easily be sucked into the rear mounted engines of the DC-9 and result in the catastrophic loss of those engines. Years earlier, on a Dallas take-off, a cap did let go. It knocked a hole the size of a cannon ball in the wing flap and sent a huge chunk of rubber through the engine. The engine survived with minor damage but it could have been much worse. I had no intention of tempting fate again.

Al heard my complaints and then asked to speak to the People's Express mechanic who shared United's operations area. People's Express was an airline that started up in the 1980's, peaked early, and then slipped into bankruptcy, never to be heard from again.

The mechanic spoke briefly to Al, put the phone down and ran outside to look at our aircraft. Shortly, he returned and whispered something into the mouthpiece. Then he handed the phone to me.

"The tire's fine," said Al.

"You can tell from 900 miles away?"

"The tire's fine," he repeated. "We see tires like that all the time. Just bring it home."

At this point in my career, I enjoyed slightly more than a month's experience as a DC-9 captain. But between Mike and me, we had over twenty years of airline operating knowledge. Neither of us had ever seen a tire cut up like this one.

I told Al that I wasn't going to accept the airplane until that tire was replaced. He grunted and hung up the phone.

I had drawn a line in the sand and I was prepared for the consequences.

At the moment, though, we didn't even know our status. No one had cancelled the flight or given the passengers any idea when it might be operating. No one had arranged for any maintenance for the aircraft. No one gave us any guidance as to what was expected of the crew and when. We were in limbo.

About an hour after my conversation with Al, I was on the ramp, slowly walking around the right side of the airplane, killing time. As I passed underneath the tail and moved to a position where I could clearly see the left wing, I noticed a torrent of fuel running down the side of the fuselage and cascading onto the concrete. It was in the area where the main wing spar attaches to the fuselage. Obviously this airplane had been smacked pretty hard.

I ran up into the cockpit and turned off the fuel boost pumps in an attempt to depressurize the fuel system and stop the leak. Then I went inside and called our flight dispatcher. To hell with Al Wilson.

The dispatcher immediately grasped the significance of what I was telling him.

"I'll send a maintenance team on the next flight to Sarasota," he said. "They'll give the airplane a hard landing inspection, fix the fuel leak and change the tire. Will you and your crew ferry the airplane to St. Louis when it's ready?"

"Sure," I told him. "Just tell the maintenance guys not to call me until the airplane is ready. I don't want to be waiting around the airport in the middle of the night if I don't have to."

"Agreed."

I briefed my crew on the current plan and released them to the hotel. I stuck around for another hour with the station manager, repositioning the airplane to a remote area. Then I went to the hotel, grabbed something to eat and went to bed.

The phone rang at 3 a.m. The airplane was ready to go.

I dialed the rooms of the other crew members and told them to meet downstairs in half an hour. By 4 a.m. we were at the airport discussing our newly repaired aircraft with the three mechanics who had flown in from St. Louis to do the work. They had replaced the tire, inspected the airframe for evidence of landing damage and repaired the fuel leak. They were planning to fly back to St. Louis with us, the ultimate testimony to their repair work. By 6 a.m. the airplane was parked at Gate C-1 in St. Louis, ready to be incorporated into the daily flight schedule. I boarded an early morning flight to Chicago and went home.

The next day, Sunday the 20th of January, I was back in a hotel in St. Louis, on reserve. The phone rang early in the afternoon. It was Al Wilson.

"I looked at that problem tire of yours. It was no big deal. I'm concerned about what's going to be said on tomorrow's company-wide conference call about the cancellation of that Sarasota flight and the stranding of 110 people."

"Well," I said, "talk about the fuel leak. That was sufficient to cancel the flight."

"Aw, that was just an inspection panel that needed to be tightened down."

"Al, they're going to play the Super Bowl this afternoon," I said. "The Monday morning quarterbacking for that starts tomorrow, too."

He hung up. There was no doubt that he was thoroughly pissed at me, but I didn't care. I put in a call to the head of the pilot's union and sketched out the situation. He told me that he'd take care of it and I never heard any more about the incident.

In subsequent flying for both TWA and American, I came to appreciate the difference in philosophies between large and small airlines. Neither TWA nor American would have quibbled about replacing a tire that one of its captains questioned. I know that Al had the best interests of the airline at heart, but safety rules are written in blood. I had no desire to make another entry.

14

Mergers

The 1980's were known as the decade of greed. Corporate raiders roamed the land, terrorizing corporations, extorting "greenmail," pillaging equity and turning it into personal pocket change. My favorite poster of the era pictured a little old lady in a pink dress, cowering in fear and clutching her tiny purse. The caption underneath the poster read "If You Steal Her Purse, You're a Criminal. If You Steal Her Pension, You're a Hero!"

Trans World Airlines, a once grand, 'round the world carrier, had forgotten its mission. Management had, in the name of diversification, invested airline assets into corporate subsidiaries like Hilton Hotels, Century 21 Real Estate and The Canteen Corporation. But it had neglected the modernization of its fleet. When the airlines were deregulated in 1978, TWA lost its competitive edge and its market share began to erode. Corporate raiders began circling the weakened company in hopes of turning the remaining assets into personal plunder.

Frank Lorenzo had made a successful run at Continental Airlines, eviscerating the unions and creating a low cost competitor. Terrified that TWA was Lorenzo's next target, TWA's unions courted Carl Icahn, a lesser evil at the time, to rescue TWA from Lorenzo's clutches. It turned out to be the equivalent of asking the fox to guard the chickens. Icahn extorted concessionary contracts from the TWA pilots and mechanics and attempted the same from the flight attendants. When they refused and went on strike, he replaced them.

TWA shared a hub with Ozark Airlines in St. Louis. In the interest of eliminating competition, Icahn purchased Ozark in 1986, extracted the Ozark equity and added the resulting debt to the TWA balance sheet. Like it or not, I was about to become a TWA pilot.

When the merger was announced between TWA and Ozark in February of 1986, the working pilots of both companies were pleased. We had had a friendly competition through the years, flying to many of the same domestic destinations and we shared jumpseat privileges. I would often have a TWA pilot sitting in my cockpit, hitchhiking home. The pilots of both companies were represented by the

Airline Pilots Association (ALPA) and were governed by the same set of rules and bylaws. The merger of the two individual pilot seniority lists would be administered according to the ALPA merger policy set up for that purpose.

ALPA was a labor union representing strong-willed, opinionated individuals who identified more with the management of a multi-million dollar corporate enterprise (an airliner) and less with salaried workers. It was a tough group to represent. In recent years, ALPA had been slow to recognize the potential threats to the piloting profession that deregulation presented and was outmaneuvered in labor-management disputes. Lorenzo, for example, had broken an ALPA-led strike at Continental and had replaced the unionized pilots. It was one of many situations that had weakened ALPA and highlighted its lack of leadership and strategic vision.

The ALPA merger policy was a document that outlined the specific criteria to be used when combining multiple pilot seniority lists. Because seniority is of paramount importance to a pilot group, it is inevitable that disputes will arise as positions on the combined list are negotiated. The merger policy, at its simplest, is an attempt to arrange seniority based on the experience level of the individuals. For example, the two main criteria for establishing experience were 1) the date the pilot hired on with the airline and 2) the amount of time he had spent as a pilot for that airline. If he had been furloughed for a period of time, or had taken personal leaves of absence, the time that he was away from the airline was deducted from his total "time in service."

The Ozark and TWA pilot groups were as different as the fleet of airplanes that they flew. Ozark pilots flew only narrow-body aircraft: the DC-9 or MD-80. The TWA pilots flew both narrow-body and wide-body aircraft: MD-80 and Boeing 727 narrow-bodies and the Boeing 767, the Lockheed 1011, and the queen of their fleet, the giant Boeing 747.

TWA had hired a tremendous number of pilots beginning in the mid-1960's and ending in the early 1970's. In accordance with the boom and bust cycles of the airline industry, those pilots hired in 1968 and subsequent years had endured lengthy furloughs, sometimes up to 12 years' duration. Many of TWA's airplanes required a third cockpit crewmember, a flight engineer who monitored aircraft systems but didn't actually fly the plane. For those pilots unlucky enough to have been hired at the end of TWA's last expansion program, they were required to serve for up to seventeen years as flight engineers before being promoted to first officer. And that's when they weren't on furlough status. Through no fault of their own, their careers had been miserable disappointments.

Ozark, on the other hand, had a fairly young work force. We had our senior pilots with over twenty-five years' experience, as did TWA, but our growth had been slow and steady. We would add a couple of airplanes and a few new destinations each year and hire accordingly. While Ozark didn't fly the glamorous, widebody aircraft, at least we didn't have the entry level flight engineer position in our cockpits. Every Ozark pilot began his career as a first officer, sharing the flight duties with the captain and accumulating invaluable experience.

When it was announced that Ozark and TWA were about to become one, big, happy family, the two pilot groups immediately began posturing. The Ozark guys saw an opportunity to fly larger airplanes at greater rates of pay and the TWA pilots looked longingly at mitigating their ugly careers by moving into the captain seats of our airplanes. It was about to become a major problem for ALPA to sort out.

The major sticking point between the two groups was the "time in service" section of the merger agreement. If that were included in the negotiations, the TWA pilots would be at a severe disadvantage because of the cumulative furloughs that many of them had suffered.

In the end, Goliath triumphed over David. ALPA National decided that the 3500 TWA pilots were more valuable than the 550 Ozark ones and allowed the TWA group to have its way. The "time in service" measure of experience was set aside and the seniority lists were merged solely on the "date of hire" of the individual pilot at his respective airline. The resulting document, limited only by temporary implementation delays, removed a group of experienced Ozark captains and replaced them with new TWA "student captains."

Once upon a time, ALPA had fought the good fight, challenging airline management to treat its pilots with respect and to provide adequate remuneration. In the accident-plagued 1930's and '40's it fought to create a national air transportation system that was safe for both passengers and pilots. But by now, ALPA had turned into another labor union, more intent on self-preservation than fighting for just causes or even living up to its own policies and by-laws.

During the months that it had taken to merge the Ozark and TWA seniority lists, Frank Lorenzo had taken over Eastern Airlines and had provoked another union-busting strike. ALPA was assessing each working crewmember at the other airlines (United, Delta, TWA, Ozark, Northwest, etc.) to provide strike benefits for the Eastern Pilots.

It finally occurred to me that I was paying several hundred dollars monthly to an organization that was representing everyone but Ozark. I stopped paying the Eastern assessments. A few months later I received a letter from the national treasurer of ALPA, ironically, an Ozark pilot. He gently chided me for getting behind in my assessments and recommended that I accelerate the payments. I responded with a scathing letter reminding him of the shoddy treatment that ALPA National had provided the Ozark pilots during the TWA merger, contrary to ALPA's official policy, and I resigned from the union.

His letter of reply reminded me that union resignation was a serious situation. He indicated that my resignation would be held in abeyance for thirty days so that a union representative could counsel me. No counseling ever took place. I received a notice thirty days later declaring that I was no longer a member of the union.

During the summer of 1986 it seemed that every time I went to work, I would hear of some additional dire consequence of the merger. Ozark captains were to be demoted to first officer, Ozark first officers were to be furloughed without regard to system seniority, Ozark pay and vacation benefits were to be slashed to reflect the TWA concessionary rates. Someone would always ask the rhetorical question: "Can they do that to us?" And the answer was always "Yes." And they did.

One day I was standing before a secretary's desk in the TWA office spaces underneath the terminal of the St. Louis Airport. I was dressed in the uniform of an Ozark captain. A friend had told me about a little yellow booklet that explained the TWA computer system and mentioned that it was available for the asking. As the secretary handed me a copy of the booklet, her eyes jumped to something happening behind me and her face went white. I turned to see a dis-tinguished looking middle-aged man, in full stride, approaching me with six other well-dressed men in suits following behind and in step.

"Come with me, young man," said the leader.

"What did I do?" I asked in mock alarm.

"No, no, I just want to talk to you," said Buck Pratt.

Buck Pratt was the TWA Chief Pilot of the St. Louis domicile. Silver haired and imperious, he had served in supervisory positions for the bulk of his career. He had very little experience actually flying the line, but he did look and act the role of the Chief Pilot.

Captain Pratt ushered me to a seat across from his impressive desk and his assistants took seats around the perimeter of his large office. I was the only one in the room who was in a uniform, albeit a foreign one, but I was quite sure that everyone there was a supervisory pilot of some kind.

Initially, the meeting was cordial. The check pilots quizzed me on some of the operating procedures and policies of Ozark Airlines. Each airline develops individual procedures for operating aircraft consistent with the manufacturer's and FAA guidelines. Buck and his boys spent some time with me comparing TWA's methods to Ozark's. It was a friendly group of pilots talking about flying, a favorite pastime of mine.

With an authoritative wave of his hand, Captain Pratt suddenly dismissed his check pilots and settled back in his chair, studying me. I could sense that his mood had changed.

"I'm not a member of ALPA," he began, "But from where I sit, it looks to me like the "red and white" pilots have the "green and white" pilots by the balls."

He was referring, of course, to the respective paint schemes of TWA and Ozark.

I could feel my anger begin to bubble up from deep inside me. I tried to keep my voice low and calm.

"If TWA plans to use the Ozark pilots to produce revenue for the corporation, it had best treat us fairly," I said. "We will have long memories."

For an uncomfortable, silent moment, we glared at each other. Then his phone rang. He told me that it was his boss in New York. With another imperious gesture, he dismissed me.

"Shut the door on your way out," he commanded.

To this day, I regret *not* slamming that door off of its hinges. Welcome to TWA.

From the standpoint of the green and white pilots, the merger between TWA and Ozark was a disaster. The green guys were to be restricted from flying the TWA large airplanes for ten years. Thereafter, we would be metered into them according to an arbitrary formula. We could continue to fly the Ozark fleet in our current status but after three years we would revert to whatever flight position our seniority on the combined list would allow. After fifteen years with Ozark Airlines, half spent as a first officer and half spent as a captain, my new TWA/Ozark seniority would entitle me to be a flight engineer!

On October 7th of 1986, Dave Woznicki and I were flying a three day trip with overnights in Baltimore and Cleveland. On the third day, October 9th, we had one more shuttle to Chicago from St. Louis, after which I would be leaving on vacation. We landed at O'Hare into a strong westerly wind that was gusting to over 35 miles per hour and taxied to a TWA gate manned by TWA ground personnel. We were about to discover the pitfalls in operating an aircraft when the procedures of two airlines are in conflict.

When the ramp agent signaled that the nose gear chocks were in place, I shut down both engines, flipped off the passenger seat belt sign and told the flight attendant to open the forward boarding door. I set the parking brakes because of the gusty winds, responded to Dave's reading of the final check list and then the two of us went downstairs into operations to secure the paper work for our return flight to St. Louis.

When we walked back to the airplane, I noticed that the chocks were properly placed on both sides of the nose gear tires and that the wind didn't appear to be much of a factor in the gate area. When I sat down in my seat, I released the parking brakes and returned the airplane to the normal gate configuration used by Ozark. Because of the many short legs that we flew, it was policy to chock the wheels and then release the aircraft brakes to enhance cooling of the tremendous heat energy that builds up in the brake assemblies after stopping a hundred thousand pound airplane on a short runway.

In the middle of the passenger boarding stream, a few minutes later, I heard the voice of one of our flight attendants cry out in alarm. I glanced up from what I was doing and looked out my cockpit window. Either the jetway was moving away from us or the airplane was rolling backwards! I slammed on the brakes and the airplane stopped, but not before the open boarding door came in contact with the frame of the jetway.

Apparently, someone on the ground crew had removed the nose wheel chocks without getting permission from either Dave or me. I found out later that TWA's standard procedure dictates that ALL aircraft at the gate WILL have their parking brakes set. The ground crew was expecting us to be using TWA's procedures when, in fact, we were still operating under Ozark's.

I stepped off of the airplane to examine the passenger door. It was obvious that the hinges had caught on a metal post and had absorbed the entire weight of the aircraft as it rolled backwards. We tried to close the door but the hinges were too badly bent to allow the door to seat properly. A squadron of mechanics and a handful of supervisors descended on us from nearby duty stations but it was obvious that there was no quick fix. The flight was cancelled and all of our passengers were accommodated on another flight about an hour later.

While waiting for maintenance to decide what they wanted to do with us, I filled out a debrief report explaining what had happened and why. A TWA supervisor asked if he could make a copy of the completed report and I agreed. Eventually, someone authorized maintenance to force the door closed to allow us to ferry the aircraft to St. Louis for repairs. Four large mechanics muscled the door into position and then Dave, the three flight attendants and I flew the empty airplane home. We parked at the Ozark hangar in St. Louis, I filed my debrief report in operations and then I caught a flight back to Chicago and home. I felt pretty crummy about the whole incident. Damaging an aircraft is a mortal sin in the aviation community. It certainly didn't leave me with a warm and fuzzy feeling as I began my vacation.

The following Monday morning, my phone rang. It was one of the Ozark flight managers who had read my debrief report and wanted more information. It seems that a copy of the report had arrived at TWA headquarters in New York shortly after I wrote it. The TWA corporate honchos were having difficulty understanding why an aircraft at an O'Hare gate would be boarding passengers without having its brakes parked. It appeared to be a blatant example of crew irresponsibility.

Of course, there was a simple solution to the entire incident. The flight manager, or his boss, could have explained to New York that it was our procedure to park the way we did. But at this stage of the merger between TWA and Ozark, the flight managers were jockeying to keep their supervisory jobs and nobody wanted to go out on a limb to explain away some damage to an airplane and the cancellation of a flight.

The flight manager, in a very friendly way, requested that I write a letter expanding my explanation of the incident. I smelled a rat. Somebody was fishing for additional incriminating information.

Jim Walters was the Ozark ALPA safety representative. I called him at home and explained the situation. He agreed with my assessment that New York was probably out for blood, my blood. He suggested that I write him a letter explaining the entire incident and then promised to hand carry it to New York and personally represent me. The fact that I was no longer a member of the union mattered not at all. Jim was a friend, a fellow Ozark pilot, who understood completely where I was coming from.

The letter that I produced described the entire situation and went on to quote page numbers and procedures in the Ozark flight manual. I sent it to Jim and he fulfilled his promise. He called me later to ease my mind and I thanked him for his efforts. Surprisingly, Ozark never published any sort of advisory to its pilots warning of the differences in procedures between the two airlines. Several times during the next couple of months, commuting to work, I would be standing in the cockpit of an Ozark DC-9 parked at the same gate in Chicago that Dave and I had used. I'd glance over at the parking brake handle on the captain's side of the cockpit. The brakes were invariably off.

◆   ◆   ◆

Initially, the plan was to operate Ozark and TWA as separate entities, coordinating flight schedules and eliminating the duplication of the two route systems. But then someone decided that it would be more economical to combine the pilot work force as soon as possible into a cross-trained unit that used identical cockpit procedures.

By December of 1986 the Ozark name was dead. We were using the TWA radio call sign to identify our flights even though both pilots in the cockpit were Ozark and the airplanes were still painted in Ozark colors. In fact, the airplanes were beginning to shuttle to a paint facility in St. Petersburg, Florida, to replace the green and white with TWA's colors. The Ozark pilots were slated to begin procedural training to learn the TWA method of flying with a target date of May, 1987, for the complete integration of the two pilot groups.

Over the next four months, all of the Ozark pilots completed a training syllabus that included four days of ground school and simulator sessions practicing normal and emergency procedures utilizing the TWA checklists. Some time after the ground school, a TWA check pilot sat on our jump seat one morning on our way to Chicago, observing our compliance with the new check lists and procedures. He was an easy-going fellow with low expectations and he pronounced us safe and ready for the crew integration.

Every pilot I talked with had a very low stress introduction to the TWA cockpit procedures, with the exception of my old buddy from the Fairchild days: Paul Walsh. Paul had been flying a trip from one of the smaller Midwestern cities to St. Louis one afternoon, when a commuting TWA pilot requested a ride to work on the jump seat. Paul launched into a tirade about TWA pilots, their unholy merger and their crummy cockpit procedures. He refused him the jump seat and grandly insulted him in the process. Guess who turned out to be Paul's line check airman a couple of months later? Instead of a quick and easy two leg line check, Paul got four days of close inspection.

When my monthly schedule for July of 1987 was awarded, I was paired with my first TWA first officer. His name was Bill Compton. Bill was an ALPA representative, currently serving on the negotiating committee. He was thoroughly involved with Carl Icahn and his New York investment bankers and was convinced that Icahn had grand plans for TWA. It took Bill some time to realize that Icahn's plans for TWA only involved the enrichment of Icahn and not the expansion of TWA. Bill went on to become the leader of the anti-Icahn faction, and eventually rose to the presidency of Trans World Airlines. But in July of '87, he was my copilot and we got along famously. In fact, when we reported for that first trip, we were pleasantly surprised to discover that we each had a copy of the current issue of Barron's Financial Magazine tucked under our respective arms. At least we knew that we had some common interests.

An incident occurred when I was flying with Bill that highlighted the differences between our personalities. We were on the ground in Chicago when an FAA maintenance inspector stepped into the cockpit and announced that he was going to give our aircraft an inspection. His credentials were authentic so I wished him well and went back to my cockpit duties.

A few minutes later he returned to say that he had found something improper with our safety equipment. Maintenance inspectors frequently find insignificant items to criticize. I think that it's partly job justification.

"Show me," I said.

He pointed to the shoulder straps on the forward flight attendant jump seat.

"They're twisted," he said.

"They're all like that," I replied.

A long pause.

"Captain, I'm telling you that there is something wrong with the safety equipment on your airplane and that is your attitude?"

I could feel my face getting red and my anger rising. Bill was standing nearby and had heard the entire exchange.

"I suppose that we could have our maintenance people look at it," he offered.

Bill stepped into the cockpit, picked up the radio microphone and requested a mechanic. When he arrived, I pointed out the offending shoulder straps and waited.

"They're all like that," said our mechanic.

The FAA inspector didn't have much to say after that. I had to chuckle, though, appreciating how much more diplomatic Bill was than I am. I'm sure that diplomacy served him well on his rise to the top.

◆   ◆   ◆

Under the terms of the combined Ozark-TWA pilot seniority list, I was now junior to the first officers I was flying with. They were prevented from assuming the captaincy because of the three year freeze that was part of the merger agreement but it was very obvious that they were anxious to move me aside and ascend to their rightful place in the cockpit. None of the TWA first officers who shared my cockpit had as much experience as I did, because of their years of furlough and as flight engineer, but they were older than I and anxious to make up for lost time. They always performed their cockpit duties professionally, however, and most were competent pilots. But it was uncomfortable flying with someone whose stated goal was to replace me.

The TWA pilot group had been heavily recruited from the ranks of military pilots. Because of a temporary pilot shortage, the aviators seeking employment in the late '60's had been given their choice of airlines. Many of the most qualified had chosen TWA because of its preeminent position as an international and domestic carrier. It had been a poor choice. Ozark, as a group, had far fewer military pilots and had recruited heavily from the ranks of general aviation. The TWA guys referred to us as FLAPS: Fucking Light Airplane Pilots.

In August of 1987, I was scheduled to fly a five day trip with a first officer named Hal Seaman. About an hour before departure time, I stepped over to the load planner responsible for producing our flight documents and asked to see our paper work. He told me that my first officer had already picked up the papers some time earlier. In a ramp office crowded with many pilots I didn't know, I had no idea who Hal Seaman was and where the flight documents were. I walked over to the crew scheduler's desk and asked him to page Hal Seaman on the public address system.

A huge bear of a man several years older than I, shuffled over to me and grudgingly shook my hand. It was obvious that he was not thrilled to be going flying with me. I asked him if he had the papers.

"Yeah, I've got them."

"Well, can I see them?"

The flight release and weather documents are issued by the flight dispatcher and signed by the pilot in command. The dispatcher and the captain share responsibility for the safe operation of the flight. The first officer usually stores the paperwork, but only after the captain has had a chance to familiarize himself with the pertinent information about weather conditions, aircraft mechanical problems, airport facilities, etc.

I followed Hal over to an area in the ramp office where he had the papers spread on the counter. About four or five of his buddies silently stood over me like vultures as I read through the documents and then signed my name on the flight release. I returned the papers to Hal's custody, told him that our airplane was parked at gate 34 and that I'd see him on board. I took my leave of his happy group thinking that this was going to be a miserable five days of Hal Seaman.

I was sitting in the cockpit when he arrived. He thrust his heavy flight case onto his seat while he removed his uniform coat and hung it on the bulkhead. He threw his beat-up hat behind the crew oxygen bottle, lifted his flight case into its holder and dropped into the first officer's seat like a 220 pound sack of shit. He started unpacking his books and assorted other tools, throwing them around in a display of passive-aggressive hostility.

I needed some way to break the ice. We had to be able to function as a crew, a safe crew, or we were going to have to terminate this flight before we ever got off the ground. I noticed that he was wearing an F-4 Phantom tie tack.

"Who did you fly Phantoms for?" I asked.

"The United States Navy!" He fairly bellowed.

I had recently read a wonderfully accurate, but fictionalized account of naval aviation during the Vietnam era titled *The Flight of the Intruder*.

"Have you read *The Flight of the Intruder*?"

"Yeah, I read it. Damned accurate," he said.

"How do you know it's accurate? Were you over there?"

"Naw, but I've got a lot of friends who were. And they told me that it was all true."

"Well," I said, "Your friends were right."

"How would you know?" he sneered.

"Because I was over there. I flew A-7's."

"Who did you fly A-7's for?" he asked, mildly interested.

"The United States Navy!" I shouted back at him.

Hal and I got along just fine after that. He was a big, gruff bear of a man with a heart of gold. A true family man, his world revolved around wife, children and his farm. Some years later, a sweet young lady, with dreams of becoming an airline pilot, stopped Hal in an airport.

"Excuse me, sir," she began, "What's it like to be an airline pilot?"

"Do you like sleeping alone?" he bellowed. "I spend half the month away from my wife and I don't like it!" That wasn't quite the response she was looking for.

On another occasion, I was flying with a TWA first officer who insisted on screaming his checklist responses to me. I stopped mid-checklist and asked him why he was screaming at me.

"I'm used to sitting back in the flight engineer's seat in a 727. I had to scream to make myself heard by the pilots up front."

"Well, Ron, you've got a window seat now so you can tone it down just a bit."

One of the things that I took for granted when I flew with Ozark copilots was their assumption that I knew what I was doing. By virtue of the fact that I had been around the airline longer than they had, they knew that my competency had been tested. I didn't feel that I had to justify my authority. It was just the opposite with the TWA first officers. They were universally senior to me and that made my credentials suspect. But we were all pilots, after all, and we usually found common ground and became friends. Personally, I never resented the fact that the TWA pilots had petitioned to steal our captain positions. That's just tough negotiating. I objected to the National ALPA condoning and permitting it. I resigned from that organization because they treated some members better than others.

◆   ◆   ◆

As some of the TWA pilots began filtering into the DC-9 captain seats, some disturbing situations occurred. Kenny Webb's incident was typical, but terrifying.

Kenny Webb was a baby-faced Ozark first officer with a solid background in aviation and many years and flight hours in the DC-9. He just looked terribly young. One day he was flying with a newly-minted TWA captain who had spent the bulk of his career flying large airplanes on international routes. He had never been a captain before and this was his first taste of glory.

As Kenny and his captain made their first approach and landing of the trip, Kenny was performing the duties of the "non-flying pilot" while the captain descended for the landing. The captain had reduced the throttle to flight idle, commanded that the gear and flaps be lowered and was flying the glide slope to the runway, decelerating to landing speed. Kenny fidgeted in his seat, watching the airspeed decrease. He knew that it takes precious moments for a jet engine to react from the idle throttle position and he was wondering when the captain was going to stop the decay of the airspeed by adding power to the engines. As they got closer to the ground and the airspeed got dangerously low, Kenny couldn't wait another moment. He crammed both throttles up and grabbed the flight controls. He flared the airplane just in time to prevent a crash, but the aircraft struck the runway harder than normal.

Deceleration was routine and they taxied clear of the runway. The captain stopped the aircraft on the taxiway, set the brakes and turned angrily towards Kenny.

"Why did you do that?" he demanded.

Kenny was angry also.

"I have a real aversion to landing in the grass short of the runway," he said.

"I had the situation under control," said the captain. "I had the auto throttles on. I was just waiting for them to engage."

"There ARE no auto throttles on this airplane!"

They taxied to the gate and the passengers deplaned. When everyone was off, the flight attendants stormed into the cockpit and demanded to know what had happened on final approach. After hearing the story, they decided that they were not going to make the return trip to St. Louis unless the captain agreed to let Kenny do all the flying. Humiliated, he agreed.

◆   ◆   ◆

The MD-80 is a newer version of the DC-9 but its electronic flight guidance system is radically different from the DC-9's traditional cockpit instrumentation. The MD-80's electronic improvements provide for a more automated all weather landing system. The system is capable of flight guidance at very low visibilities but its use requires entirely different cockpit procedures.

Ozark segregated its fleet of DC-9's and MD-80's, permitting its pilots to fly one aircraft or the other. In the interest of economy, TWA decreed that the MD-80/DC-9's would be flown by the same pilot group and it would be their responsibility to respect the differences between the two airplanes and apply the appropriate procedures. The FAA allowed the intermixing of the two aircraft because they shared a common type rating. In other words, the FAA decreed that it was legal for the pilots of an airline to operate both the DC-9 and the MD-80. Whether it was appropriate to do so would depend on the number of passengers who lost their lives in landing accidents. "Legal" and "appropriate" are sometimes mutually exclusive concepts.

When an aircrew flies an airliner to a runway that is shrouded in fog, there is a point somewhere above the runway where the captain must decide if he has the required flight visibility to land the airplane. If he does not, he must execute a "missed approach" to return to a safe altitude above all terrain. The procedures for executing that missed approach are radically different depending on the aircraft being flown.

For example, a missed approach in a DC-9 requires the pilot to simultaneously disconnect the auto-pilot, apply maximum allowable power to the engines and pull back on the yoke to rotate the aircraft to begin a climb. In the MD-80, the procedure is automated and the pilot is only required to push a button on the throttle assembly and then monitor that the aircraft adds power, rotates and climbs. If a pilot were, for example, to mistakenly apply the automated missed approach procedure of the MD-80 while flying the DC-9, the aircraft would very likely strike the ground before he realized that it was not responding. To complicate matters, Ozark flew about five variations of DC-9's with two radically different cockpit configurations. All perfectly legal, but hardly appropriate.

In the fall of 1987, I attended MD-80 transition school. The ground school lessons delineated the differences between the MD-80 and the DC-9 and provided a cursory refresher course in aircraft systems. Randy Mayhood, an Ozark first officer, and I were paired together for two training sessions in the MD-80 simulator with an instructor pilot named Roger Meyers. Roger was an easy-going TWA pilot in his middle fifties who stressed flying the simulator as a crew, helping each other to get used to the new flight guidance system. The instructor pilot who administered our check ride, however, was a humorless individual whose personality was as obnoxious as his lack of flying ability. He insisted that each pilot function independently and refused to allow us to coordinate the flight duties. After the check ride was complete, I couldn't get away from him soon enough.

Some months later I flew a fully automated approach and landing into Salt Lake City. The airplane and its electronic landing system performed marvelously. I just observed as the MD-80 flew itself onto the runway. On touchdown, I selected reverse thrust on the engines, applied the brakes and taxied off of the runway. Then I was lost. The fog was so thick that the control tower had to send out a truck to lead us to our parking spot. It is ironic that a hundred and thirty thousand pound airplane flying an approach at 140 miles per hour can navigate to and land on a specific patch of concrete that is completely shrouded in fog, but then once there, can't locate its assigned parking place a hundred yards distant.

For the next three years, my trips were usually five day combinations of various versions of DC-9's and MD-80's, sometimes alternating every couple of legs. My first officers were, for the most part, TWA guys who were senior to me and anxious to move me and my fellow ex-Ozark pilots out of our captain's seats. In April of 1990, they got their wish. April 2nd, I completed my last trip as a captain and donned the slick-billed hat of a first officer, in accordance with the terms of the merger agreement. At least my seniority had improved to the point where I no longer fit into the ranks of the flight engineers. For the next six years I would fly with many of the same TWA pilots who had served as first officers for me. But now they were in command.

About a dozen of the Ozark captains who were downgraded to first officer contracted medical problems that prevented them from flying. Real or imagined, they removed themselves from flight status and fought to receive a retirement based on medical disability. Two of my six classmates from Ozark days medically retired rather than endure the humiliation of demotion. One extremely volatile friend died of a heart attack in his shower. Several others, captains and first officers alike, quit TWA in disgust and sought airline jobs with United, American, US Air, FedEx or UPS, giving up years of seniority.

For the most part, the TWA captains I flew with were mature, competent airmen who enjoyed the simple hands-on flying of the DC-9/MD-80 operation. But there were two exceptions.

John Grace (not his real name) was a gracious, serious TWA pilot in his mid-to-late fifties, just a few years away from mandatory retirement age. He had been an international first officer and flight engineer and was used to the slow, deliberate pace of long distance travel. The New York to Paris route, for example, required some activity at the take-off and landing phases but most of the trip was spent sitting and eating on the seven hour enroute segment.

I met John before the beginning of our five day trip. He shook my hand warmly and told me that this was his first trip as a captain. He said that he was grateful to have such an experienced first officer but that he couldn't allow me to make a take-off or landing during our trip because of the company rule that required a new captain to do all of the flying for his first 100 flight hours. I told John that I understood and that I would be quite content to perform the duties of the "non-flying pilot".

Our first leg on the evening of March 20th, 1991, was from St. Louis to Ontario, California. The taxi and take-off were normal and we settled into the four hour cruise segment of the trip, flying toward the setting sun, dining on crew meals and chatting with flight attendants who were temporarily hiding from their passengers. For John, it probably seemed as comfortable as his international days but was even more satisfying because he was finally the captain of the ship, the guy with the four stripes on his uniform coat who makes the decisions and basks in the glory.

The descent into Ontario is a busy proposition. After sitting for four hours at 35,000 feet with minimal radio intrusions, we were about to enter the Los Angeles traffic control area with the nonstop radio chatter from over-stressed air traffic controllers routing airplanes to a dozen busy airports. Each airport has its own arrival routes and crossing restrictions that inbound pilots are required to precisely observe.

The rule of thumb that MD-80 pilots use to plan their descent dictates that the altitude in thousands of feet be multiplied by three to figure the distance required for the descent. For example, a 35,000 foot cruise altitude would normally require 105 miles across the ground for a descent to a landing. If conflicting traffic prevents initiating a descent from cruise altitude at an appropriate distance from the destination airport, either the pilots must employ a high drag device, like wing spoilers, to increase the rate of descent or they must fly additional air miles to bleed off the excess altitude when authorization for the descent is finally given.

Our descent clearance from air traffic control was late. By the time we were overhead Palm Springs, 55 miles from Ontario, we were still above 24,000 feet and John was struggling to make a crossing restriction of 14,000 feet, 21 miles ahead of us. He knew that we had a descent/approach checklist to complete and some other preparatory landing items to accomplish, but his mind had gone blank. On my own, I finished the checklist items and flipped on the Fasten Seat Belt sign. I figured our weight for landing, set the speed bugs on the airspeed indicator and hit the button on the thrust computer to the Go Around position. Then I turned my attention to helping John get the airplane in compliance with air traffic control instructions. I pulled on the speed brakes to increase our descent rate and to slow our airspeed. I changed the frequency on John's radio and coached him into turning toward the radio beacon that marked the beginning of the 26R ILS approach. John was still about 10 miles behind the airplane! I coached him into extending some slats and flaps and into slowing to around 200 miles per hour. By the time the landing gear came down, he had caught up enough to call for the landing checklist and I felt that he was back with me. The landing was adequate and we taxied to the gate, shut down the engines and went to the hotel for the night. I felt like I had earned my pay.

The next afternoon we were in the TWA operations office at the Ontario Airport, looking over the flight documents and weather reports for our return trip to St. Louis. I noticed that thunderstorms were forecast to arrive in St. Louis at the same time that we were. I suggested to John that he set aside the fuel load that the dispatcher had planned and completely fill our fuel tanks. He agreed and we left Ontario with enough fuel to fly all the way to New York and beyond.

It was getting dark as we approached Missouri and I could see that thunderheads were indeed beginning to crop up all around us. By the time we checked in with St. Louis Approach Control, thunderstorms at the field had slowed the arrival rate to the runway and the controllers put all of the inbound aircraft into holding patterns to buy themselves some time. We were holding about 50 miles west of the city at 15,000 feet but the storms were building near us. Twice, we had to request to move our holding pattern away from the turbulent, lightning-infested clouds.

Then air traffic control (ATC) issued one of its famous gloom and doom proclamations.

"All aircraft be advised that we don't anticipate any arrivals for the next hour because of thunderstorms at the field."

John was beside himself. He demanded that I get an ATC clearance to Des Moines, our alternate airport for St. Louis.

"Hold on, John," I suggested. "We're sitting here with 13,000 pounds of fuel, enough to last for over two hours. Why don't we wait it out for awhile? Every one is going to leave and we'll be in great position to slip into St. Louis with any small break in the weather."

"No, I'm not comfortable with that. Get me a clearance to Des Moines."

I told ATC that we wanted to go to Des Moines and we climbed to 24,000 feet for the trip. An hour later I was coaxing John into a Midwestern airport that he had never seen, fighting turbulence and gusty winds in the lower altitudes. We had no sooner landed and begun our taxi to the ramp when Des Moines operations called to say that St. Louis was wide open and that they wanted us refueled and back there ASAP.

As soon as the airplane was parked, I went downstairs into operations and found a secluded corner. I counted slowly to 25, trying to get my anger under control. John was a nice man but he had no business in the cockpit of an airliner.

Des Moines refueled us in record time and we were soon taxiing to Runway 30R. Lightning was still flashing in the night sky around us but the storms were some distance from Des Moines.

"I can't do this," John said to me.

I looked over at him and saw that his hands were shaking.

"Will you fly it to St. Louis?" he asked me.

"Sure, John. No problem."

I flipped the flight guidance switch to the number two position, told the tower that we were ready and we started our take-off roll. The rest of the flight was uneventful and free of all weather problems. When we got to St. Louis, the flight that we were supposed to have flown to Baltimore had left with another crew and we were sent to New York for the night.

Our five day trip turned into a six day marathon but at least John and I alternated the flight duties. On the sixth day he shook my hand and thanked me for my help. I never saw him again. Either he retired or he reverted to being an international first officer. I don't know. I think he knew he wasn't cut out for the fast-paced domestic operation of the MD-80.

In January of 1992, I was flying with another brand new captain, Ed Spray (not his real name). On the first day of our five day jaunt, we had flown to Cleveland and then spent the night in Little Rock, Arkansas. The next day found us on the way to Kennedy Airport in New York and then on to Washington National Airport for the night.

Washington National Airport (renamed Ronald Reagan Washington National Airport) is located on a jut of land in the Potomac River across from and south of the cluster of important buildings and monuments that represent the seat of our national government. Washington National Airport should have been closed years ago. The longest of its three runways is only 6869 feet, barely adequate for jet operations. The Washington Dulles Airport, by contrast, boasts twin parallel runways over 11,000 feet in length and an intersecting runway 10,500 feet long.

Washington National exists for the convenience of powerful people. Its departure and arrival corridors are heavily restricted and most flying is limited to the airspace immediately above the Potomac River. One of the visual approaches for a landing to the south actually requires the flight crews to follow the twists and turns of the river, almost flying between the buildings on either side of the river, to a point where a low altitude turn can be made to line up with the runway. It's a testimony to the skill of the flight crews that in recent years only one flight, Air Florida, has had the temerity to crash and burn while attempting to comply with National's restrictions.

On January 23rd, late in the evening, Ed and I took off from Kennedy for Washington National, operating TWA flight 873. Seated between us in the cockpit jumpseat was an FAA air carrier Inspector whom I had never met. The weather in Washington was forecast to be awful: rain, fog and low ceilings. At least the temperature was above freezing so we didn't have to worry about ice on the short, wet runways.

When we checked in with the Washington air traffic controllers, it was obvious that they were extremely busy. The radio chatter was non-stop. We were assigned a heading to intercept the inbound course for the LDA DME Runway 19 approach with glide slope. This particular approach is flown directly over the Potomac River, but at a 45 degree angle to the landing runway. In other words, when the pilots descend below the fog at 700 feet above the ground, they must visually acquire the landing runway and make a 45 degree turn to the right to line up with it. If the visibility is poor, which it was this night, it makes for a hairy low altitude final approach.

Ed was flying the approach but he was too high and still too fast. I suggested that we lower the flaps and gear and get the airspeed under control. Still ten miles from the runway, he had plenty of time to get the airplane configured for landing but he was slow to make the necessary changes. Eight miles from the runway we should have been at 2300 feet and descending, but we were still above 3000. I completed the landing checklist and continued to monitor Ed's progress on the glide slope. By now his airspeed was within a few knots of ideal but he was still too high on the glide slope.

"You're high, Ed," I prompted him.

No response.

"You're still high on the glide slope, Ed!"

We were approaching the point where we were supposed to make our turn to the runway. I could see the approach lights off to the right but we weren't in a position to make a safe landing. Wisely, Ed decided to go around.

He added "go around thrust" and I raised the flaps to 15 degrees. I told the tower that we had missed the approach and waited for their instructions. The controller was pissed. We had just complicated his life a little more. He told us to climb to 3000 feet and fly a southerly heading. Eventually, he worked us back into the stream of airplanes that was lined up for the same approach that we had just attempted.

A few minutes later, the gear and the flaps were down and we were lined up on the approach course that would take us to our turn point. Again, Ed was flying above the glide slope. I had visions of repeating the mistakes of the first approach.

"Ed," I shouted, "Get down on the glide slope!"

He pulled the throttles back a bit but not nearly enough.

"Ed," I was fairly screaming. "GET ON THE GLIDE SLOPE!"

This time he made the correction and when we approached the turn point he was able to see the runway and make the landing. I was relieved to be on the ground but I was beginning to wonder what the FAA inspector was going to say to us when we got to the gate. First officers are not supposed to scream at captains in flight.

Ed parked the brakes, shut down the engines and told the flight attendant to open the passenger door. I could see that the FAA inspector was collecting his stuff. I held my breath.

"Good crew coordination," he said. Then he stepped into the moving stream of deplaning passengers and disappeared.

I'm certain that many of the FAA air carrier inspectors appreciated the potentially disastrous consequences of merged airlines but the decision to permit it was made at pay grades substantially above them. Since no fatal accidents occurred as a direct consequence of the merger between TWA and Ozark, the FAA was never forced to justify its merger policies. But the FAA struggled to reconcile the diametrically opposed twin missions of its charter: Promote aviation and Regulate aviation. Legal and appropriate, difficult and sometimes conflicting concepts.

15

Strangers

My brother, Lee, once created a security incident aboard an airliner. October 19th of 1993, I was still flying as a TWA first officer. John Winslow was my captain on the evening flight, TWA Flight 588, from New Orleans to Atlanta to Washington Dulles.

We were parked at the D Concourse at Atlanta's Hartsfield Airport and I had just completed a "welcome aboard" announcement on the PA when I heard a commotion in the galley behind me. A passenger, bent on forcing his way into the cockpit, was being physically restrained by a couple of the flight attendants. Their faces white with fear and anxiety, they were intercepting what appeared to be a potential highjacker.

"Do you know this guy?" one of the ladies asked me.

"Yeah, he's OK. He's my brother."

Lee was a vice president for Scientific Atlanta at the time, traveling to Washington on business. He had recognized my voice on the PA and wanted to come up and say hello. When he started forward, perhaps a little too enthusiastically, the flight attendants had grabbed him. After a short cockpit visit, Captain John put Lee and his partner in first class and we gave them our crew meals to snack on.

On October 1st of 1996, my TWA seniority finally allowed me to return to captain status, where I remained for the rest of my career. I'd like to say that there was some socially redeeming higher purpose in having had to serve those six years and five months as a first officer again, but it was simply due to the vagaries of merging one airline into another. At any rate, I was glad to be back in the left seat, where I could solve flight problems in my own way and set the tone for the interaction with the crew. I flew with some wonderful TWA captains during that period, like John Winslow, but I worked with a few jerks, too.

◆   ◆   ◆

The typical airline passenger probably doesn't give the composition of his crew a second thought. He or she probably assumes that the flight crew has been trained as a unit, that all the members of the group have known each other for some time and that they have flown together on countless occasions. In reality, the exact opposite is much more probable.

The quintessential airline crew is a collection of strangers. The smaller the airline, the more likely it is that a few flight attendants or pilots might actually know each other on any given crew. But for a large company, like American or United, strangers are the norm. It is a testimony to airline training and standardization that a group of diverse individuals can unite, sometimes on short notice, to become that efficient and safe operating unit that everyone takes for granted.

One of my preflight rituals as a captain was meeting and greeting the crew members on the assigned day of a flight. Each crewmember was required to sign in via computer at least an hour before flight time and be on board the aircraft shortly thereafter. Personally, I enjoyed being the first on the scene. I liked to begin the "nest-building" operation as soon as possible, laying out all the books, headsets, glasses, hand towels and personal incidentals on my side of the cockpit. I'd adjust my seat for elevation and pitch, test the emergency oxygen and communication gear and then I would step back into the cabin to meet the crewmembers as they arrived.

Even if a flight attendant looked familiar, it was always protocol to say your name and refresh his or her memory when he or she stepped on board. The arriving crew member would, in turn, say his name and usually offer a handshake. Most of us used our short term memory to keep the names of fellow crewmembers fresh, but that was just on a daily basis. A couple of days after the termination of a trip, it was the rare fellow who could remember where he went on the previous trip, much less who went with him. An individual crew member has hundreds of acquaintances within the airline, but very few good and close friends.

After the first officer arrived on the scene, we'd spend a few minutes with the basic sort of get-to-know-you stuff and then he and I would have to get down to business. There would be time to explore each other's personality and history in cruise flight when the work load drops off. For the moment, we have computers to program, routes of flight to check, FAA clearances to decipher and countless other distractions that all have to be dealt with during the last minutes before closing the boarding door.

By the time we started the taxi process, I had a good feel for who the first officer was and I usually had made some mental notes pertaining to items that I wanted to explore further with him. 99% of the young men and women I worked with were intelligent, motivated and well-trained. Cockpit crew coordination demanded that we adapt our personal styles of flying and make an attempt to become comfortable with each other. From having spent many years in that right seat, I know that the most difficult part of being a first officer is respecting the captain's personal rules and idiosyncrasies. In my role as captain, I tried to establish a very professional and efficient working environment that was open to suggestions but as stress-free as possible. Interpersonal rivalries have no place in the cockpit of an airliner.

One Sunday morning, three flight attendants and I left a downtown Dayton hotel. Our first officer was supposed to meet us at the airport, inbound from another flight. When it became obvious that he was a no-show, I called crew scheduling, the department responsible for matching crews to flights. Someone had dropped the ball and had neglected to assign and transport a qualified first officer to this particular flight. Passengers and crew were stranded until we could locate another first officer. The scheduler did volunteer that there was a first officer in the Dayton hotel who was planning to work a flight later in the day. If I could talk him into leaving early with us, we'd have our complete crew.

I called him from the airport and probably woke him up. I explained our need and he agreed to help us out. When he showed up about an hour later, I couldn't believe my eyes. He was huge! Probably not over six feet tall but he had to be approaching three hundred pounds. He looked a little like the Pillsbury Dough Boy. Later, in the cockpit, when the workload had stabilized, I asked him what he liked to do when he wasn't flying.

"I like to eat," he said. I knew that I was working with an honest man.

Another first officer who became a good friend was Gerry Spear. He was a solidly-built, ex-hockey player from Minnesota who was a joy to work with. He was a very capable pilot and just fun to be around.

Gerry was once sitting in the St. Louis Airport, killing time between flights. He heard a commotion some distance away and looked up to see a man running full speed from another man who was lying on the ground. The fellow on the ground was a police officer who began shouting for someone to stop his escaping prisoner. One of our captains, a big man, tried to intercept the fugitive but the prisoner just ran over him. Watching all of this, and seeing the prisoner getting closer and closer, Gerry timed his full-body block and exploded into the fleeing man. He knocked him backwards and came to rest lying on top of him. The prisoner had the wind knocked out of him and was gasping for breath. Gerry saw a Glock 9mm pistol come up along the side of his head and heard the DEA agent say "Thanks. I'll take it from here." Gerry was awarded a certificate from the FBI and DEA for stopping a fugitive. Sometime later, he told me that what really motivated him to stop that prisoner was when he saw what he did to the first pilot who had a chance at him. Neat guy.

I think that in 31 years of airline flying, half of which was spent as a captain, I only encountered two first officers who were major problems. One was a name-dropping bullshit artist whom I found intolerable. If he could have flown as well as he could talk, he would have been a "super pilot." Put that down to a personality conflict. The second one was the son of one of our captains.

I met Bob before the beginning of our two day trip together. He had the physique of a weight lifter and seemed like an easy-going sort. The first airplane we were going to use on the afternoon of November 13th, 2000, was coming from the maintenance hangar in St. Louis where it had been undergoing a series of scheduled maintenance checks. I warned Bob to double check all of the switches in the cockpit because the maintenance guys frequently position oddball switches that we seldom use. Shortly after we had settled into the cockpit and had begun running our preflight checks, Bob turned on the cabin oxygen system and immediately blew down all of the emergency masks in the cabin. Maintenance had left the oxygen mask switch in the emergency position and when system pressure was applied, the masks came down. Of course, the position of the oxygen switch was a checklist item, something that should have been checked each and every time that a new crew assumes responsibility for an airplane. But that particular switch is "always" in the normal position and it's easy to overlook.

Maintenance advised us that it would take some time to repack all of the oxygen masks in their overhead brackets, so we packed up all of our flight gear and walked back into the terminal. Thirty minutes before our scheduled departure time we were given another airplane for our flight to Knoxville. I had planned to take a few moments to talk to Bob about what had happened but as soon as we reentered the terminal, he whipped out his cell phone to discuss the problem with his father.

By the time we left Knoxville, we were back on schedule. We operated flight 583 to St. Louis and then flight 537 to Sioux Falls, where we spent the night.

The next morning it was Bob's turn to fly. Cleared for take-off, I taxied the aircraft into position on runway 21 at Sioux Falls and told Bob that he had control of the rudder pedal steering system. I pushed the throttles up to take-off power and called out the v-speeds as we accelerated. At the appropriate rotation speed, Bob pulled back on the yoke to establish the twenty degree deck angle that would begin our departure climb. Somewhere around ten degrees nose up, his seat let go. He slid all the way back to the aft limit of the seat track where he could no longer reach the controls. Fortunately, my seat held. I told him that I had control of the airplane and I completed the take-off.

With some difficulty, he muscled his seat uphill and locked it into place. When he was comfortable, I relinquished control of the airplane and he continued the climb to altitude. Every pilot has experienced a runaway seat at least once in his career but it usually happens early and seldom happens again. It just takes a moment to test the lock sometime before take-off to prevent the loss of control at a very critical time.

Without the hint of an apology, Bob climbed to 33,000 feet and put the airplane on the autopilot. Then he reached into his bag and pulled out a copy of "USA Today" that he had scavenged from the hotel.

It's always been a pet peeve of mine when a first officer pulls out reading material in flight. With the aircraft moving through the sky at speeds approaching ten miles per minute, the least we can do is look out the windows for potential problems. Besides, how many jobs are there where you actually get paid to look out the window?

Using my best attempt at tact, I told Bob that I would make a deal with him. I wouldn't read the paper in flight if he wouldn't. It took him a few seconds to get it. Then he crumpled his newspaper in disgust, stuffed it into his bag and pouted. I was beginning to look forward to the end of this trip.

I had never met Bob before but I was vaguely aware of his father. His father had flown the DC-9 and the 727 before losing his medical license to a hearing problem. Bob was acting as if he had some sort of special status as the son of a TWA captain.

We landed in St. Louis, terminating flight 565 and originating flight 582 to Raleigh. Shortly, we were airborne again, cruising at 29,000 feet southeast-bound to the Carolinas. I was flying the leg this time. Conversation between Bob and I had all but died. He was also looking forward to the end of the trip.

Typically, conversation in cruise flight is fairly slow. By the mid-point of a trip you usually know everything you care to about your copilot's history and family life and conversation becomes an effort. You're forced to listen to the radio chatter in your headset, trying to pick out your flight number in the unending stream of air traffic control banter. Cockpit conversation is like talking to someone who's listening to someone else. It's not unusual to fly for half an hour without saying anything at all to the person sitting along side of you.

Maybe because I was flying the airplane this leg, Bob felt that he was relieved from traffic watch. He pulled out his bid sheets and began planning his next month's flight schedule. By now my fuse was getting short. I told him to put that crap away and do his job. He looked at me with homicide in his eyes but he grudgingly complied.

At the gate in Raleigh, Bob jumped out of his seat and disappeared. I finished the last of the cockpit duties and then stood in the doorway thanking the passengers as they filed off of the aircraft. In preparation for the next flight, I descended the jetway steps into the warmth of the Raleigh sunshine and slowly walked around our airplane, performing the traditional pre-flight inspection.

When I returned to the cockpit, I noticed that Bob had left his uniform coat draped across his seat. His ID card was still attached to the coat but he was nowhere in sight. I went down the steps and walked across the ramp to the door leading to operations. Bob was there, standing at the counter, looking at the paperwork for the next leg.

"Did you walk across the ramp just now, Bob?" I asked him.

"Yeah, I did."

"Where's your ID card?"

He glanced quickly at his shirt and then said, "It's on the airplane."

I figured that I had chipped at him enough for one day. I turned to the station manager who was working over some papers at a desk within earshot.

"Trudy, would you please explain to this young man why no one is allowed on the ramp without an ID card?"

"Oh, my gosh," she said.

She went on to explain to Bob how the FAA had been on a tear lately. Any unauthorized people in the vicinity of an airplane, or just on the ramp, without proper identification and authorization would generate a $10,000 fine. She was in no mood to have ten thousand dollars deducted from her station operating budget and she emphatically communicated that fact to Bob.

After she had gone, I figured that it was time to have a chat with Bob. I have always believed in discussing and resolving cockpit conflicts as they occur, rather than letting them fester into official reports or after-the-fact accusations.

"Bob, we need to talk," I offered.

"I have nothing to say to you." I was surprised by his hostility.

"You would rather talk to the chief pilot?"

"I have nothing to say to you."

"Ok," I said. "Have it your way."

We flew back to St. Louis in silence. I wrote a quick report to Roger Mason, our chief pilot. Entitled "Five Dumb Mistakes," I sent it via email and went home.

Roger caught me the next week. He told me that he had had a little chat with my uncooperative first officer. Bob had been a festering problem for Roger for some time, a candidate for discipline or dismissal. Roger warned him and then arranged for the professional standards committee of the union to talk with him. Hopefully, Bob got the message. He did, some time later, find me and reluctantly apologize. I never flew with him again.

One of the first items of interest at the beginning of every trip was the crew list, a roster of names of all crewmembers working an individual flight. If none of the names on the list was familiar, you knew that you'd be working with strangers. If one or more of the names elicited unpleasant memories of past personality conflicts or disagreements, there would be an elevated level of tension before the trip even began. If, however, you recognized one or more of the crew members from a past, pleasant trip, you could assume that this trip would be pleasant also.

Early one morning I walked aboard a DC-9, threw my suitcase behind the captain's seat and started unpacking my flight kit. Olivia Smith, a petite African-American flight attendant with a dazzling smile, stepped into the cockpit to say hello.

"Good Morning, Rog," she said. "I was glad to see your name on the crew list this morning."

She told me that she was going for coffee and wanted to know if I'd like a Starbucks. I offered to buy but she said that the treat was on her. She was just glad to be flying with a familiar face.

By the time she returned with the coffee, the first officer and I were chatting in the cockpit. Olivia handed me the tall Starbucks while the first officer looked on with envy.

"How do you rate?" he kidded me. Familiarity has its rewards.

On the 25th of February, Tom Duncan and I were operating flight 571 to Sioux Falls. About 13 miles from the airport, descending through 4,400 feet and still in the clouds, a formation of three Canadian geese slammed into the nose of our aircraft. My initial reaction was that we had struck the 3500 foot TV tower that was just below us. Then I saw the blood on the windshield.

A Canadian goose is not a small bird. The larger ones can weigh fifteen to eighteen pounds and, when splattered by an airplane at 290 miles per hour, they can cause massive damage to an airframe or an engine.

The first goose in the formation struck high on the center windshield and left a bloody trail heading aft. The second goose penetrated the black nose cone protecting the aircraft radar transmitter, slammed into the firewall just below Tom's right foot and exited, in liquid form, through the closed nose gear doors. The last goose struck full force on Tom's side window; actually overcoming the pressurization holding the window closed. It packed the window frame with blood and guts and sprayed blood all over Tom and the wall behind him. The noise of the collisions carried all the way to the passengers seated in the aft of the airplane.

John McGowan and Maria Howell, friends from Ozark days, were the flight attendants working in the back. They told me later that when my voice came on the PA assuring them and the anxious passengers that our sturdy DC-9 was still in fine shape and that the landing would be routine, they were relieved. Because of past experience together, they knew that they could trust me. They were grateful for the familiar voice.

Generally, crews prefer to stay together for the duration of a trip series. The mutual trust between cockpit and cabin crews can only evolve after the successful completion of a certain number of flights. Once, during the boarding process, a group of flight attendants told me that they had three separate unruly passengers who were causing problems. Since the flight attendants were new to me, I had to determine whether the passengers were the source of the problems or if the flight attendants were being unreasonable. Prior working knowledge of the cabin crew would have been extremely useful in making that determination.

Between flights, the pilots and flight attendants often camp out in the first class section of the airplane, trading stories and getting to know each other. By and large, I found the flight attendants to be very caring individuals who enjoyed their jobs and did their best to put their passengers at ease. There were always a few with an ax to grind but it was a minority.

When John Gray's book, *Men are from Mars, Women are from Venus,* came out, I found some extremely useful techniques for dealing with the female flight attendants. According to John Gray, women don't want men to solve their problems. They just want men to listen to their problems.

Typically, just before departure, an exasperated flight attendant would come into the cockpit with a list of complaints: commissary had neglected to supply enough plastic cups, for example, or there weren't enough first class meals. Maybe the liquor kits had not been replenished, the guy sitting in 4B smelled badly and the floor in the galley needed to be mopped. She would be adamant that her problems be resolved before she shut the boarding door.

I would stop what I was doing, turn so that I could clearly see her and just listen to her. When she had gotten everything off of her chest, I'd offer to do whatever I could to make her feel better. Invariably she would say, "Oh, I think we can handle it. I just needed to vent." Then she would return to her galley to re-attack her problems.

On the rare occasions that the flight attendants wanted something fixed, I would do my best to accommodate them, coordinating maintenance or commissary servicing. But at the very minimum, they liked knowing that their complaints were taken seriously.

On several occasions a gate agent would come into the cockpit with doubts about boarding a problem passenger. Since the flight attendants were the ones who have to deal with the passenger if he were allowed to board, I always liked including them in the decision-making process. Once, an agent informed me that the other passengers in the boarding area were becoming alarmed with the strange hand gestures and mumblings of a fellow passenger. I went out to the boarding lounge to observe the man in question and then returned to hold a brief meeting with the flight attendants. One male flight attendant, the owner of a black belt in Karate, promised me that all would be well. We accepted our problem child and the flight proceeded uneventfully.

Once upon a time in Houston, a gate agent came aboard to warn me of an abusive and emotional woman who claimed to be a teacher. She was berating all of the agents for various offenses. They had decided that she was emotionally unstable and unfit for transportation. I grabbed my head flight attendant, a tall, distinguished, African-American man named Fred, and the two of us went out to the boarding area. I was immediately grateful for Fred's presence. The lady in question was a well-dressed, middle-aged, African-American woman who was standing some distance from the ticket counter, isolated from her fellow passengers.

I introduced myself as Fred stood silently by my side. I explained that I had been told that she was a problem, but that I wanted to hear her side of the story. She calmly explained that she had been having a very bad day and that she had gotten off on the wrong foot with one of the gate agents. She accused the agent of being abusive and hostile. She told me that she was a teacher and assured me that she would not be a problem.

I, in turn, assured her that we could accommodate her and that she would be welcome. Then the dam broke. She sobbed uncontrollably for an uncomfortable period while Fred and I watched in silence. Finally, I interrupted her and asked the obvious question.

"Why are you crying?" She couldn't answer and continued to sob.

I pulled Fred down the boarding ramp until we were in private.

"What do you think, Fred?"

"I don't want her."

We shut the boarding door and left town.

Now and then I had a little fun at the expense of a flight attendant…..and vice versa. I was visiting with a pretty girl between trips, seated in the first row of first class. She complained that she could never find Mr. Right. I excused myself and went down onto the ramp. I found about eight guys (mechanics, agents, baggage loaders and pilots) and asked them to talk to the brunette sitting in first class. One at a time, they all filed aboard the airplane and introduced themselves as "Mr. Right."

A flight attendant once called us in flight to report that there was a strange vibration in the galley. The first officer, who admired the current crop of young ladies, volunteered to step back into the galley to identify the source of the vibration. Flight attendants have a keen sense when something is not right with an airplane. Many of them have flown for years on familiar airplanes and when something is out of the ordinary, they notice immediately.

Before the first officer got out of his seat I noticed that the center fuel tanks had almost completed their transfer. While the last few gallons are being pumped, the fuel pumps often cavitate, i.e. they suck in air with fuel and produce a noticeable vibration in the airframe.

I flipped off the center fuel pumps as the first officer stepped into the galley. Soon, he was back to report that the vibration had stopped. As he was strapping himself into his seat, I flipped the center pumps on again. Almost immediately, the flight attendant called to let us know that the vibration was back. I let the first officer make one more trip to the galley before I confessed…

One of the most courageous flight attendants with whom I ever worked was a lady named Claudia Masters. She had been stricken with rod and cone dystrophy at the age of 40 and began a slow journey that would result in almost complete blindness. Ten years later, her color vision was permanently impaired and she saw everything as variations of fuzzy shadows. Still, she continued working, performing her safety and service duties so efficiently that fellow crew members couldn't detect her handicap. She even earned a commendation for her participation in the emergency landing and evacuation of a flight into Albuquerque. Eventually, her vision problems were discovered when she couldn't read the questions on her annual emergency training test. She wouldn't have had any trouble with the answers...or the practical aspects of her job. But her inability to read forced her into medical retirement.

Anyone who has ever been an airline crew member has accumulated abundant material for short stories. There is something unnatural, but exhilarating, about enclosing a group of people in a metal cylinder and propelling it through the air. The passengers often exhibit behavior influenced by claustrophobia, fear of flying or nicotine withdrawal. Crew members are usually physically attractive (at least in the cabin) and in possession of strong, independent personalities. Add a dash of romance or a hint of danger and the routine airline flight becomes an adventure. Or, at least, entertainment.

16

Passengers

No discussion of airline flight operations could be complete without mentioning some of the more interesting passengers who have flown with us through the years. Travelers who step aboard an airliner trust and expect that the cockpit crew will fly them to their destination as efficiently and as comfortably as is humanly possible. Of course, the *primary* expectation is that the pilots won't make a mistake and kill them in the process. Relinquishing control of their destiny to the flight crew is easier for some than for others. Some passengers feel better only after having personally quizzed the captain and first officer about their sobriety, fatigue and experience, usually in that order. To the flight crew, however, intrusive and insulting questions that insinuate incompetence are more tedious than comical. Personally, I always preferred the first time flyers who would sneak shyly into the cockpit to admit their nervousness.

"This is the first time I've flown in an airplane," one attractive older lady confided to me.

"Me, too!" I told her with a grin. Her horror only lasted for a moment.

I was delighted to have bright-eyed kids show up in the cockpit, with or without their parents. I'd let them experiment with the auto-pilot or flip some switches and then I would quiz them on the direction and geography of the day's flight. It was always a challenge to answer their questions on a level that they could understand, but I loved encouraging them and trying to relate their studies of mathematics and science to the flight at hand. Some children, at the insistence of parents or well-meaning flight attendants, had visited the cockpit to the point of boredom and had absolutely no interest in the foreign display of dials, switches and gauges.

One morning, I sauntered through the cabin as the aircraft was being refueled and cleaned. When I saw a lad of about 12, sitting alone, playing a portable video game, I asked him if he would like to come up front and see the cockpit.

"Nah," he said. "I've been up there lots of times." The product of divorced parents, his routine included shuttling between different cities, sharing custody between estranged parents and two sets of grandparents. He was a frequent, and very bored, flyer.

Occasionally, celebrities would visit the cockpit to chat or make a request. Congressman Richard Gephardt was a frequent commuter on TWA between St. Louis and Washington, D.C. He was a friendly, gracious man who always rode in the coach section of the airplane. He was a great friend to the employees of TWA in their struggles during the bankruptcy process. Senator Robert Kerry, on the other hand, traveled in first class and glowered at anyone who threatened his privacy.

Red Skelton, the genial television comedian, once popped his head in the cockpit during passenger boarding. He was wearing a gold-colored, wool sport coat that complimented his ruddy complexion and his graying red hair.

"I'll be in row 3 if you need me," he said with a twinkle in his eye. Then he was gone. What an instantly likeable man!

Phyllis Diller begged the use of our cockpit coat closet to hang the full length animal wrap that she was wearing as an outer garment. During that flight, I kept glancing over my right shoulder at the monstrosity riding with us. I just had the feeling that the damn thing was watching me.

Airlines often pander to coach passengers during flight delays by offering free cocktails and extra snacks. Of course, the freebies only show up when the airline is the cause of the delay. If air traffic control or bad weather is the problem, the delay is deemed to be an act of God and the airlines keep their booze to themselves. Personally, I interpreted the rules fairly loosely and distributed free liquor whenever I could. I would just sign the form that the flight attendants produced at the end of the flight, authorizing free drinks, and I was never questioned. I had no way of knowing whether the passengers drank all of that stuff or if it disappeared into flight attendant purses and suitcases. In the long run, it probably didn't matter.

Years ago, I was operating a series of Ozark flights in and out of St. Louis. The weather had alternated fog and rain all day. By early afternoon, we were once again parked at the main terminal at St. Louis Lambert Airport, boarding another load of passengers. We were late and our prospects for making up time and returning to our published schedule were slim.

A few minutes before departure, an irate but well-dressed man in his forties forced his way past the flight attendants and into the cockpit. I became aware of him when he bellowed into my ear.

"You're late," he announced. "The least you can do is offer us free drinks!"

I turned to look at him and was instantly angry. He stood in our cockpit, hands on his hips, belligerent in body language and tone of voice.

"I've been giving away free drinks on my flights all day," I calmly told him. "And I had planned to give them away on this flight, too. To everybody except you."

For a moment his face betrayed his shock. Then, without a word, his ego thoroughly deflated, he slunk back to his seat. I motioned the chief flight attendant into the cockpit and instructed him to offer free cocktails to anybody who wanted one——except for the man who was just up here. He agreed and told me later that the man in question was pouting and staring out his window when the flight attendants passed through the cabin with their beverage cart. He wouldn't even look up, much less answer questions about soft drinks or peanuts.

One evening, inbound to Austin, Texas, one of the flight attendants called me on the intercom. He informed me that there was a problem passenger, a belligerent, inebriated cowboy who was becoming more difficult as the flight progressed. He assured me that, for the moment, everything was under control but he couldn't guarantee the future. Since we were only 30 minutes out of Austin, I requested maximum speed to the airport and set about getting the aircraft on the ground.

The landing was uneventful. We cleared the runway and began the long taxi to our assigned gate at the new Austin airport. The intercom chime sounded and the flight attendant announced that his problem cowboy was out of control, walking through the cabin and pulling his belongs out of the overhead storage bins. He refused to heed the instructions of the flight attendants and was bouncing off of his fellow travelers in a drunken haze.

I called ground control on the radio and requested that the airport police meet us at our gate. I parked the aircraft about 50 yards from our final destination and waited, allowing time for the cops to get into position. I warned the passengers to remain seated until I released them. A few minutes later, ground control called to tell me that the cops were ready and we continued our taxi. As soon as the engines were shut down and the wheels were chocked, the largest black cop I have ever seen tapped on my cockpit window. I slid the window open and briefly described our situation. Then the flight attendants opened the main boarding door and three large cops stormed aboard, ignoring our still-seated passengers. Our drunken cowboy left in handcuffs and spent his first night in AUS in the local jail. You don't mess with Texas. And that was *before* 9/11.

Prior to 9/11, it wasn't wise to cause a disturbance on an airliner in flight. After 9/11, it was potentially suicidal.

As a result of tightened security in the aftermath of the attacks on New York and Washington, most of the face-to-face, in-flight interaction between cockpit and cabin crews was terminated. Before 9/11, a captain or first officer could stroll through the aircraft in flight, stretching his legs, visiting with the flight attendants or passengers, consulting on passenger medical problems or other concerns. At the request of one of our flight attendants, I once sat with a terrified lady for almost twenty minutes, explaining the physics of flight and the source of each little vibration or bump as we cruised thru the bright sunlight at 35,000 feet.

Flight attendants would often pop into the cockpit to vent about fellow crew members or problem passengers, flirt with young first officers or just hide from their responsibilities for awhile. That culture was killed along with the butchered flight attendants of the United and American flights on September 11, 2001. Cockpit doors are now reinforced and bullet-proof and are not to be opened routinely in flight. If flight attendants are assaulted in the cabin, the crew of the fortress cockpit is forbidden to render assistance. They are required to sacrifice the cabin crew for the greater good of the survival of the aircraft and passengers. No wonder that the expendable flight attendants suffer from a lack of *esprit de corps*.

One night, enroute to Hartford, Connecticut, the intercom chime sounded. I picked up the handset to speak to one of the three ladies working in the cabin. I recognized Sarah's voice and knew immediately that she was upset. Sarah was a slender, attractive brunette in her 30's with a couple of small children back home in St. Louis. From the tremor in her voice, I knew she was scared.

Sarah described two passengers: a petite blonde and a tall, well-built athletic man, both in their 20's. The blonde, who claimed to be engaged to the young man, had been making excuses for his behavior since the beginning of the flight. At first, when one flight attendant commented on his lethargy, the fiancée claimed that he was over-tired. Then, when he became agitated after take-off, the blonde claimed that he was a white-knuckle flyer, extremely fearful but only temporarily affected. Only later, when the man became disruptive, loud and very vulgar did the blonde admit the real problem. Apparently, the young man was subject to psychotic episodes, had been off his medications for a dangerous interval and was returning to Hartford to be treated by a familiar psychiatrist.

I asked Sarah what sort of behavior she was observing. She described loud, angry and profane verbal tirades. At times, the man would throw anything within his reach to punctuate his rage. There was a running argument that was escalating between the man and the woman, and it was threatening to overwhelm the rear of the aircraft. Many passengers were fleeing to the forward sections of the airplane while the flight attendants attempted to restore order.

I told Sarah to enlist the help of several good-sized men and brief them on the situation. I cautioned her not to incite a riot by getting them involved unless it was absolutely necessary. I didn't want a replay of the Southwest Airlines situation where a group of passengers smothered a fellow passenger who was unruly.

I told her that, at the moment, we were over Dayton, Ohio, and our eastbound track would pass over Columbus, Pittsburgh, Harrisburg, Philadelphia, Allentown and New York. Any of those cities could provide police assistance. I promised her that if she felt sufficiently threatened, I would get the airplane on the ground on very short notice. It was up to her to make that decision since she was the lady in harm's way. She promised to check in with me every ten minutes so that I would have a running commentary on the situation.

As we proceeded eastbound, Sarah's reports were timely, but varied. The little blonde was speaking very low to her boyfriend, engaging him in conversation and trying to preoccupy him with small talk. Then his temper would flare and he'd be throwing magazines and plastic cups and screaming.

I didn't want to divert to another airport unnecessarily because of the inconvenience to the majority of our passengers, but if Sarah had asked, I wouldn't have hesitated. Thirty minutes out of Hartford, she told me that the situation was fairly stable and that she was reasonably confident that nothing terrible was imminent. I asked her what sort of assistance she would like to have waiting for us.

"Get the police," she said. "And the paramedics. This guy is pretty close to letting go."

There was quite a crowd of emergency personnel waiting for us at Gate B-5 at Hartford's Bradley International Airport. Sarah opened the forward cabin door and the passengers began streaming off the airplane, more grateful than normal to have their feet back on the ground and to have escaped the limiting confinement of our noisy airplane.

When the bulk of the group had deplaned, two cops and three paramedics charged aboard, making a bee-line for the altercation that was taking place in row 17. I followed them back to watch the show.

The female cop asked our male psycho to calm down and sit down. Just the opposite occurred. With an angry outburst of profanity, he shoved his girlfriend and moved toward the cops. That was all they needed. They quickly placed him in handcuffs and led him off the aircraft. A marvelous ending as far as we were concerned…

The percentage of passengers who misbehaved on my flights was tiny. Of the hundreds of thousands of people that I have had the honor of transporting to family reunions, business obligations, funerals, weddings or vacations, I can remember less than a dozen who were obnoxiously improper.

As a young first officer, I learned an invaluable lesson in passenger diplomacy from a captain named Frank Weiss. A decade older than I, Frank was a tall, dark, charismatic figure with an infectious smile and a voice that was simultaneously warm and commanding. One morning, we were operating a flight that originated in Chicago but made an intermediate stop in Peoria, Illinois, before continuing to St. Louis. Just before we started our engines in Peoria, ground control called to tell us that St. Louis was fogged in and that we had a weather delay of at least an hour.

Frank picked up the PA, made a short announcement to the passengers about our delayed departure and then climbed out of his seat to take a walk through the cabin. With nothing better to do, I trailed a few steps behind him.

About mid-cabin, an attractive lady in a business suit stood to block Frank's path. She announced that she was an attorney, had important business in St. Louis and had absolutely no patience or time for delays of any kind. Frank just stood there, silently watching the lady and listening to her complaints. Impulsively, he reached out and embraced her in a warm, friendly hug. Still in mid-sentence, she melted. Frank empathized that her business was, indeed, important and that he would do everything in his power to get her to St. Louis as soon as feasible. It was a moment before she could speak. When she regained her composure, she thanked Frank for his concern and apologized for her impatience. What a transformation I had just witnessed!

Unfortunately, I wasn't blessed with Frank's looks or charisma so I had to develop my own passenger-handling skills. My approach was to rely on the native intelligence of the traveling public and to always tell the truth. If an aircraft or engine system was in need of repair, I would explain the problem in as much detail as I thought necessary and then pass through the cabin, answering individual questions. If air traffic control delayed our flight for weather or excess traffic at the destination, I would explain the situation and then invite anyone who was so-inclined to visit the cockpit during the delay. I encouraged visitors to discuss anything of interest, up to and including politics and religion. Some interesting people, many of whom would not have come forward unless invited, visited our cockpits to share their thoughts, but always in a very civilized, friendly and courteous manner.

An airline captain has ultimate, and sometimes arbitrary, discretion over who will or will not be included in the passenger manifest. A discourteous, abusive passenger can be removed in a heartbeat. I've employed that option several times during my career. Conversely, someone who understands how the game is played can move mountains.

It is standard operating practice for the ticket agent to back the jetway away from the aircraft several minutes before departure time. Then he remains at the controls of the movable walkway until the aircraft begins the slow backwards push toward the active taxiway. By hiding on the jetway until the aircraft is moving, he avoids any late passengers that might arrive at the check-in podium, pleading to get on the flight. God forbid that the flight be delayed for any reason, especially if the delay could be charged against the gate agent for late passengers!

One afternoon, the jetway was pulled away from our aircraft and the agent was standing at its controls, reading a magazine, waiting for the huge tug to push us backward. A nicely-dressed man in an expensive-looking three-piece suit somehow managed to get onto the bridge from the main terminal and make his way out to the aircraft. He ignored the gate agent who tried to intercept him, dropped his brief case and threw himself on his knees at the edge of the four foot chasm separating the bridge from the aircraft. He knelt there, just a few feet from my side window, hands clasped in mock prayer, silent except for his eyes.

I motioned the gate agent to bring the jetway back to the aircraft and instructed the flight attendant to open the main door. The businessman clambered to his feet, muttered a quick "thanks" as he went by the cockpit door and took his seat. He was a man who knew how to play the game.

17

Personal

In April of 1983, Ozark Airlines, citing the pressures of competing in the deregulated airline industry, closed its Chicago pilot domicile and consigned all of the flying to the remaining domicile in St. Louis. From now on, all of my trips would begin and end in St. Louis. I was given a choice: move or commute.

The real estate market in our small, rural Illinois community was less than booming and the one realtor who looked over our property was hardly enthusiastic. By now, I was the protector-provider for one wife, two daughters and a son, all of whom had ties to the community and very little incentive to move away. It seemed logical that I should at least try the commuting option for a while and spare the family the upheaval of moving to a strange place. After all, one of the fringe benefits of working for an airline is free air transportation.

My wife was a local celebrity in the little Illinois town of Genoa. She was the church organist and a vocalist who was in demand for weddings and funerals. She possessed the star solo voice in the church choir and for over ten years taught the three and four year old children who attended the United Methodist Preschool. It was seldom that we went anywhere locally but that someone, large or small, wouldn't recognize her.

My extended family is centered in northern Illinois and my parents still live in the house in which I was raised. My wife's family is from Iowa. In the summer of 1969, she had come to California to help her sister with a new baby. I met Jo Ann at the apartment swimming pool that her sister and I shared in the Navy town of Lemoore. I was immediately stricken with her and quickly monopolized her remaining time in California.

We began a whirlwind courtship that consumed all of our free time. When Neil Armstrong was taking "his one small step for man" on the surface of the moon, Jo Ann and I were driving California route 1 from San Simeon to San Francisco. We visited Santa Barbara and stayed with my Aunt Mary who lived in a Spanish home with a breath-taking view of Los Padres National Forest and Santa Barbara Bay. We drove to Kings Canyon National Park and Yosemite for mountain hikes and picnics. I took her to the Lemoore Naval Air Station and introduced her to my trusty Corsair and some of the squadron pilots.

The remaining weeks of her California visit raced to a close and Jo was forced to return to Iowa to prepare for the next school year where she was a second year, second-grade teacher at Davenport Grade School in Ames.

After she left California, we were both miserable. I petitioned the skipper of VA-93 to authorize a weekend cross-country flight in an idle A-7 and he approved. I left California in the middle of the night and flew solo to Offutt Air Force Base near Omaha where Jo Ann was waiting. We caught a cab to the Omaha Airport and flew United Airlines to Chicago to meet my parents. We bought a diamond ring at a local jewelry store and I put it on her finger in the city park where I used to play as a kid. Over dinner that evening, at my father's table, we announced to the world that we were engaged.

That visit was terribly brief. Jo Ann and I flew back to Omaha and caught a cab to Offutt. I climbed into my Corsair and flew west as Jo drove east to Ames. Within a few weeks, I was enroute to Vietnam. Nine months and 132 letters later, I boarded another United flight from San Francisco to Des Moines, arriving June 7th, 1970. We were married a week later at her father's church in Fort Dodge. From the day I met her to the day I married her, I think we were together, in person, a grand total of four weeks.

But all of that was once upon a time…a hundred years ago…

The commuting worked well for a while. Ozark was running hourly shuttle flights between Chicago and St. Louis. On paper it would appear that the next flight between the two cities would be just a short wait but because the flights were notoriously late, the 2 pm flight, for example, would fill up with passengers who were booked on the 3 pm flight and anxious to get out of town. For a non-revenue standby passenger, it was not unusual to miss two or three flights before successfully completing the trip. Because of the tremendous time involved in coming and going, I usually flew a series of trips that lasted four or five days, thereby reducing the total number of monthly commutes to a minimum.

Since I only lived fifty miles from O'Hare, it seemed logical that Chicago should be my jumping off point for St. Louis. But as American and United, the two local giants, added flights to the Chicago market, the air traffic control delays increased and O'Hare became terribly frustrating.

One afternoon, I had completed a series of flights in St. Louis and was released to go home. I was fortunate to have secured a seat in the cockpit on a TWA flight that was already filled to capacity. As I walked down the jetway to meet the crew, the lady flight engineer of the Boeing 727 was strolling in the opposite direction. She smiled to see another crew member, obviously trying to hitchhike home.

"Don't be in a big hurry," she said. "We have a two hour ATC delay."

By now O'Hare had become a "blue sky airport." As long as there weren't any clouds in the area, the airport could handle its assigned schedule. But with weather of any kind, a two hour air traffic control delay was all too common.

By the time we did actually land in Chicago, the ATC delay had stretched to almost three hours and the in-flight holding had consumed another one. From start to finish, a trip that should have taken an hour had extended to five. I thanked the crew for the ride and began the hike to the employee bus that would take me to my car and eventually home.

The phone was ringing when I walked into my kitchen. It was Dave Burrows, the principal of the high school.

"Roger, were you on flight 210 out of St. Louis just now?"

"That was me, Dave. Where were you?"

"I was way in the back. I saw you up in the cockpit but the flight attendants wouldn't let me come up and talk to you. What in the hell happened?"

"Let me call you back, Dave. I'm a little too upset right now."

I went upstairs and took a long, hot shower. Feeling a bit more civilized, I called Dave and explained everything that had delayed our flight that afternoon. Then I told him something that surprised me.

"I'm never going to fly out of O'Hare again," I told him. "I'm going to find an easier way to get to work."

When the time came to begin my next series of trips, I drove west for two hours to Moline, Illinois, a small city on the Mississippi River. I parked my car at the Airport La Quinta Hotel and walked the ten minutes to the airport. The manager of the hotel was a jovial grandfather type whom I had met on the short crew layovers in Moline.

All of the Moline ticket agents for Ozark Airlines were friends of mine. Years of flights flown in and out of Moline had established a good working relationship with the ramp and gate personnel. In fact, it was Jim Cooper, one of the more affable and pleasant ticket agents who suggested that I give up O'Hare and use Moline as my commuting base. The Moline agents did their best to get me on the St. Louis flights so that I could go to work, sometimes even sliding me ahead of paying passengers. For the remaining years I lived in Illinois, I either drove two hours west to Moline or an hour and forty minutes north to Milwaukee. The driving miles were greater than to O'Hare, but the uncongested airports greatly reduced the frustrations of the commuting experience.

By the end of the 1980's, Ozark had been swallowed by TWA and my professional career was unraveling. Multiple corporate bankruptcies, the loss of the Ozark culture and identity, massive pay cuts and demotion to first officer created a miserable work experience. My wife was safely insulated from my professional trauma and had no interest in sharing it. She was caught up in planning weddings for our daughters and her church work. I began keeping my complaints to myself, discussing my work situation with a handful of close, personal friends.

A homebody by nature, I'm probably a strange animal to be a professional traveler. I spent so much of my working life in the large cities that I longed for the seclusion of our three acre home, surrounded by all the trees and bushes that I had planted in that ex-cornfield. I loved our peaceful, country home.

One day I asked my wife where she would like to live in retirement, still some eight years away. I had planned for it to be a rhetorical question. Her answer was immediate.

"Ames, Iowa," she said.

"Why Ames?"

She reminded me that she had been teaching in Ames before I married her and had thoroughly enjoyed the college town atmosphere. She had sung in the choir of the campus Presbyterian Church and treasured the memories of her years there. She had a list of complaints about our present home in the country and said that she wanted to live in a town where shopping and other amenities were close. And then she told me about her friends. Or lack, thereof.

She didn't feel that any of the Illinois ladies with whom she associated were of the same educational background or that they sufficiently shared her interests. That was a surprise because I always considered her to be the social animal of our family, the person who could meet someone for the first time and very shortly know that person's entire history and ancestral lineage. I was amazed that she felt so dissatisfied with the large group of people with whom she interacted.

A few years ago, Jo Ann and her two sisters had enjoyed a 17 day European excursion. The three women had toured many countries, got along famously and thoroughly enjoyed themselves. It occurred to me that perhaps the type of friend my wife needed at this point in her life was, in reality, a sister. I speculated that she needed to be closer to them. Her sisters lived in Iowa, within an hour of Ames.

I agreed to drive to Ames and look over the city. We spent a weekend exploring the neighborhoods and walking through the campus of Iowa State University, which makes up half the population of the town. We had dinner with her room-mate from her teaching days and quizzed her about the local situation. All in all, Ames seemed like a wonderful place to live, culturally alive and youthfully influenced by the University. I could very easily commute to St. Louis from the Des Moines Airport, less than an hour away. We drove back to Illinois and put our house up for sale.

In October of 1999, we moved to Ames. We had been looking for a smaller house than the four bedroom French Provincial we had built in 1973 in Illinois, but the one we found and fell in love with was actually a little larger and much more inviting with its nine foot ceilings and the airy openness of the floor plan. It became obvious that this house had been meant for us when we discovered that the outside combination of the garage door opener was the date that we were married: 0614 (June 14th). We laughed about that.

Jo Ann busied herself unpacking boxes and decorating the new house. She hosted all of the Iowa relatives for holiday gatherings and our children drove from Illinois to get a first look at the home and the lifestyle that would eventually center our retirement years. The good vibrations lasted for three months.

I came home from a trip in mid-January of 2000. Jo Ann was curled up on the couch in the fetal position, crying uncontrollably. I have seen clinical depression before and I recognized it. The combination of the long-distance move, the empty-nest syndrome, the deteriorating health of her parents, the loss of her celebrity status in the community, separation from children and grandchildren, and the complicating effects of other health problems conspired to drag her down. I assumed that with the help of a counselor and some medical intervention we could restore her mental health. At the moment, however, Jo Ann was incapable of making even the smallest decision and some of her comments appeared suicidal.

My boss graciously granted a two month leave of absence from the airline and I took over the daily household duties. By late February, Jo Ann was sleeping better but was far from whole. In March, she asked me to sit with her. She wanted to tell me something. Initially, I suspected that she wanted to tell me that she had found someone else.

"I know why I'm depressed," she began. "It's Ames. The people aren't friendly here and the church isn't anything like I remembered. I need to go back to Illinois."

I didn't know what to say. It sounded like the "grand geographical solution." Just pack up and move and our troubles won't come with us. Personally, I've always been more inclined to face life's problems than run from them. I could not embrace her logic. Ames, in my opinion, had proved to be everything that she had promoted it to be.

As the next year unfolded, she became more and more distant. There was an endless stream of counselors who would listen to her and suggest remedies. They suggested that she get a job or take a course at the University to develop a local identity. She refused because it would have limited her ability to drive to Illinois to visit our children and grandchildren.

Christmas 2000 was awful. Our children were in Iowa with us for a few days but the tension between Jo Ann and I created an uncomfortable and stressful situation. I'm sure that they were frantic to get back to their own homes and away from us.

By January, the emotional strain was taking its toll on me. Hives were a daily companion. One afternoon I noticed that my upper lip was swelling. As the afternoon gave way to evening, the swelling spread to my lower lip and accelerated. Both lips were now horribly bloated, cracked and oozing. I was beginning to wonder if I should take these symptoms more seriously. I asked Jo Ann to call the local hospital for help in diagnosing whatever was destroying my face. She refused. I could barely speak by now but I dialed the number of the emergency nurse and tried to describe the situation. The nurse's advice was to get to the emergency room as soon as possible.

Jo Ann drove me to the hospital and dropped me outside the entrance to the emergency room. I must have looked like some sort of grotesque creature from "The Blue Lagoon" when I walked into the hospital. The first nurse to get a look at me rushed me to an examining room a short distance from the entrance. She administered twin shots of adrenalin and a strong anti-histamine and wrapped me in blankets. By now, Jo Ann had found me and was responding to the lengthy administrative questions of the staff.

I was shivering uncontrollably from the adrenalin and the nurses kept piling on warm blankets. At one point, I stole a look at Jo Ann, who was now seated in a chair at the foot of my bed. Where once I would have seen compassion and concern in her face, tonight I saw only contempt. I think it was at that moment I knew my marriage was over.

I spent the night in the hospital and the next morning the swelling was almost gone. An allergist prescribed a combination of anti-histamines that were compatible with my flight duties and FAA restrictions. He told me that hives, edema, and the associated restriction in the breathing passages were commonly driven by emotional stress and that a long term solution to my problems would have to address those underlying concerns.

In February, Jo Ann began the first of many lengthy separations. She drove to Illinois and spent a couple of months with our daughter, sleeping in our grandson's bedroom. I provided her with a separate checking account and allowed her the freedom to decide what it was that she wanted.

After one of these long absences, I met her in Illinois the night before a family christening. She complained that it was impossible to improve our marriage while she was in Illinois and I was in Iowa. She said that she'd like to try another round of marriage counseling. I invited her to come home and promised to go to whatever counselor she suggested. She agreed to return on the following Sunday.

At home in Ames, I waited all day for her. There were roses on the kitchen table with a card that said "Welcome Home, Jo. I Love You." She finally arrived around 8:30 pm, walked in the door and began crying. I held her for two hours while she sobbed uncontrollably.

The next morning we saw a counselor who recommended another counselor. By July, we knew that we were going nowhere. One afternoon, she was sitting in her recliner in the family room, a familiar look of exasperation on her face. A tense, uncomfortable silence filled the room. I went over to her, hugged her knees and suggested that we just end the marriage. She thought for a moment and agreed. She stood and I embraced her. I was immediately overcome with a sudden flash-back to a happier time, a sun-drenched afternoon, when I held a long-haired beauty in a brown flowered dress. Jo Ann asked me to keep our impending divorce a secret until after the Thompson family reunion the following week. I agreed.

August 10th, 2001, I returned from a trip. It was my birthday. Jo Ann was waiting for me.

"Happy Birthday," she said. "I filed for divorce."

She moved back to Illinois to become a full-time grandmother, living near my family. I remained in Iowa, living near hers. The marriage lasted 31 years, 29 of which I'll cherish with memories of love, family and friendship. I still can't believe that two lovers, who endured wartime separations, raised and educated three children and shared such a long and intimate history, could dissolve their bonds and choose separate paths...but there are no guarantees in life, and love doesn't always last forever. When one door closes, another one opens...life goes on.

18

The Last Door

During my thirty-year airline career, I had a front-row seat for the consolidation or dissolution of many familiar brands: Eastern, Pan American, Braniff, Muse Air, Air Florida, and Frontier all ceased operations and liquidated. Piedmont, Ozark, North Central, Western, Hughes Air West, Southern, North East Airlines, Mississippi Valley, National, Republic, Reno Air Lines, and others merged into larger units.

Early in 2001, it was becoming painfully obvious that TWA could not survive as an independent entity. In spite of several rounds of employee concessions and the forgiveness of debt through the bankruptcy courts, the revenue side of the profit-and-loss equation was still inadequate.

Bill Compton, the president of TWA, announced early in the first quarter that American Airlines would soon become the parent company of TWA. Another venerable aviation icon would very shortly cease to exist. By April 1st, it was official. The collection of uniforms in my closet was about to grow larger.

That summer, TWA employees were introduced to American Airlines via training bulletins and computer courses. Pilots, flight attendants, and gate agents attended classes to learn the Sabre reservations and crew-management system. A December target date was established for the retirement of the TWA brand. Airplanes would be repainted and crews re-uniformed by January 1st. The cultural changes were coming quickly—too quickly.

On September 11th, 2001, I was at home, dressed in my TWA uniform. I was scheduled to fly a late-night trip from St. Louis to Phoenix and was planning to catch the 11 a.m. flight from Des Moines to St. Louis. As I sat down to tie my shoes, the drama unfolding on CNN caught my attention. I watched in horror as the Twin Towers of the World Trade Center descended into rubble.

The magnitude of the attack on the United States deepened with the impact of the American Airlines flight into the Pentagon and the United Airlines flight that crashed in Pennsylvania in lieu of the White House. I knew that there was no chance that my trip to Phoenix would operate later in the day, but I couldn't stay home. I drove to the airport and spent most of the morning commiserating with the Des Moines ticket agents, who were as stunned as I was.

On September 18th, after the nation's air transport system had partially recovered from the shock of 9/11, Frank Mays and I began a 4-day series of trips that would take us to New Orleans, Minneapolis, Charlotte, and other cities. We carried less than 20 passengers per flight from big city airports that resembled ghost towns. On one trip, we had a grand total of six brave souls flying with us. Clearly, the tragedy of 9/11 was going to have deep and serious consequences for the airline industry.

By spring, the furloughs of airline personnel began. At first it was just a few copilots and flight attendants who were given notice, but by summer a more ambitious plan had been developed that would release thousands of crew members and reduce the number of flights nationwide. In accordance with a contract with its unionized pilots, when American Airlines furloughed pilots by the hundreds, it was required to offer early retirement to those senior pilots who could qualify.

By virtue of the seniority system that governs airline personnel, I was now a senior captain and easily qualified for the early retirement package offered by American. Since I had invested so little time in the parent corporation, my pension from them would be minimal. However, they did offer the incentive of a year's salary without the commensurate obligation to fly any more trips. If I chose to accept the package, my last trip would occur at the end of October, 2002, but I would be paid through the last day of September, 2003. In effect, I would have 1 year of retirement at full pay before my pension began.

The last door of my aviation career had opened.

I had been dreading the changes in corporate culture that would be imposed by assimilation into American Airlines. There would be lengthy days of ground schools, followed by tedious simulator sessions and check rides to learn the American way of flying airplanes. By mid-2002, we looked like American Airlines pilots. We wore American uniforms and our airplanes were decorated in their distinctive red, white and blue stripes on polished aluminum. But the pilots in our cockpits flew using TWA procedures. And we flew as friends, familiar faces from years of fraternity, albeit at a different airline. Cosmetic changes were easier to accept than the procedural, cultural differences yet to come.

I filed the form requesting to be included in the early retirement offer. Strangely, I had few misgivings about my decision to walk away from a career years before the mandatory retirement age of 60. As opportunities had presented themselves throughout my life, I had never hesitated. Once again, I was quite certain. Retirement was an opportunity, perhaps the beginning of something yet unknown.

So it was that my last crew, Debra, Brian, Jeff, Missy and I, found ourselves in a Little Rock restaurant the evening before my last flight. The first officer bought my dinner and everyone in the crew wished me well. The next morning, in Philadelphia, on October 30th, 2002, a cleaner snapped a picture of the five of us in uniform. Framed in dark oak, it sits prominently on my desk, testifying that, once upon a time, I held the rank, exercised the privileges and fulfilled the responsibilities of an airline captain.

As a 23-year old Navy pilot, I reconciled myself to the concept that my life may be brief, and that it may end violently. That it didn't is probably more a testimony to great good luck than to personal skill and daring. As a military pilot, I survived 156 combat missions in the skies over Vietnam, and hundreds of day and night landings aboard aircraft carriers. As an airline pilot, I worked with thousands of different crew members, in good weather and bad, safely transporting millions of passengers to their destinations.

Aviation has been very good to me. It provided me a tremendously satisfying career, a wealth of pleasant memories, and a collection of harrowing tales with which to bore my grandchildren. I have been an extremely fortunate man.

◆   ◆   ◆

In March 2003, my 25 year-old son deployed to Kuwait in preparation for the war in Iraq. He was the executive officer of an armored company attached to the 4th Infantry Division of the Army. It was a tense time for my entire family. One evening, as my 6 year-old grandson watched news footage of the various elements of the armed forces preparing for the conflict, he pointed to the Abrams tanks that my son would be commanding. Then the video switched to the Navy. An aircraft carrier was shown, catapulting fighter jets into the sky, armed for battle.

"Look, Wesley," said my daughter. "Grandpa used to fly planes like that."

"No way!" said my grandson.

Yes, Wes, I did all sorts of things that you haven't yet begun to dream of. John Magee would speak of slipping the surly bonds of earth, climbing through sun-split clouds and rolling and soaring where never an eagle has flown. I did that, too, Wes. And, God, it's been fun! I'll tell you about it someday.

Bibliography

Gray, John, *Men Are from Mars, Women Are from Venus: A Practical Guide for Improving Communication and Getting What You Want in Your Relationships.* HarperCollins Publishers; 1st edition (May 1, 1992)

Magee, John Gillespie, *High Flight.* England, September 1941
Information from Web site entitled: www.skygod.com/quotes/highflight.html

0-595-33691-4